T5-AVO-722

Grannies Have More Fun

WITHDRAWN
NOSU

Grannies
HAVE MORE
Fun

VERA SMITH

Iowa State University Press / Ames

TO

Frederick G. (Rick) Smith

Kiffany Lynn Frank

Courtney Paige Kline

Vera Smith, author of *Grannies Have More Fun*, lives in Malvern, Iowa, where she writes a regular column for the *Malvern Leader*.

© 1990 Iowa State University Press, Ames, Iowa 50010

All rights reserved

Manufactured in the United States of America
⊗ This book is printed on acid-free paper

No part of this book may be reproduced in any form by an electronic or mechanical means, including information storage and retrieval systems, without written permission from the publisher, except for brief passages quoted in a review.

Authorization to photocopy items for internal or personal use, or the internal or personal use of specific clients, is granted by Iowa State University Press, provided that the base fee of $.10 per copy is paid directly to the Copyright Clearance Center, 27 Congress Street, Salem, MA 01970. For those organizations that have been granted a photocopy license by CCC, a separate system of payments has been arranged. The fee code for users of the Transactional Reporting Service is 0-8138-1818-4/90 $.10.

First edition, 1990

Library of Congress Cataloging-in-Publication Data

Smith, Vera
    Grannies have more fun / Vera Smith. — 1st ed.
      p. cm.
    ISBN 0-8138-1818-4
    1. Smith, Vera   . 2. Grandmothers—Iowa—Biography.
    3. Aged as authors—Iowa—Biography.   I. Title.
    CT275.S5595A3   1990
    977.7'03'092—dc20
    [B]   90-40296

Contents

Preface

I n keeping with all of the good luck I'd already had in my life, I felt fortunate when the first letter I ever wrote to an editor was published, given a title and picture head, resulted in a surprise check, and produced an invitation to write more. We oldsters have been bombarded with the idea that all is lost once a person graduates out of the fifties. I disagree with that theory and set out to list my reasons in that first column. Ever since 1976 I've never missed a week in filling two or three pages about interesting things that happen in our lives. The editor, Pete Graham, headed that first column with probably the only picture he had of a female senior citizen— a forlorn-looking old soul.

Grannies... Have More FUN! by Vera Smith

The whole theme of my writing was that old women don't have to appear that way. Still I didn't mind the picture and enjoyed having an audience to enlighten that young people are not the only ones to whom pleasant, good, and rewarding things happen.

When I started this little diary-like column about my life, I had no idea that so many people would read it and identify with it and that I would receive letters from every state in the nation.

Folks who move from their home states have a custom of subscribing to their hometown newspaper. Sisters and aunts and mothers clip columns they read and send them to relatives afar. I've written about life here in the Midwest. It's easy for me to write glowingly about this because of my long-standing love for the state of Iowa and the people who live here. I've kept a booster notebook from the first week I was published and received a letter from Dr. Phyllis Conner of Omaha. At the end of the eleventh year, I had the names of 6,843 persons who had written to me concerning my columns.

In the book I have eliminated all of the book reviews, recipes, and "letters from readers." The book contains all of the subjects dear to my heart.

One of my biggest thrills concerning the book is that our grandson, Bradley Frank, flew out from Colorado on his spring break last year to illustrate the book for me.

I realize that it isn't being several years over seventy that causes me to have fun. It's having good health, many interests, a loving family, and many good friends. For all of these blessings, I'm thankful.

Grannies Have More Fun

_____

Some Casual
Observations

The advantages of middle age

February 26, 1976

Sometimes I get disgusted with hearing all of the supposed disadvantages of middle and old age, and I disagree with the supposed disadvantages in nearly every way possible. There is no time in a person's life that can be more fun or carefree.

For one thing, middle-aged people have more independence (no parental interference and no live-in children for whom a good example must be set at all times).

By the time one reaches middle age, anxiety about what other people think has diminished. Middle-agers have learned that they can't please everyone even if they want to, so they may as well just relax and please themselves. This is a great time in life for those who love to read. Seldom in earlier life can they read for four or five hours a day without neglecting something or somebody else. In middle age, people can do exactly as they want.

Another nice thing about being middle-aged is that by this time people have learned not to take life so seriously. By the time people are sixty or close to it, they realize how small are some of the things that seemed to loom large at one time—for instance, worrying about a perfectly adorable child who doesn't get straight A's in school or fretting because they've bought a five-hundred-dollar bassoon for a boy who would rather shoot baskets than play a double-reed instrument. So what if your children went through a time when they avoided

4

speaking to your friends? And so what if your son, who is now a real estate tycoon, once took a winter quarter off from college to ski at Aspen for three months at your expense?

And how wonderful to be middle-aged in a time of the big wig business! Instead of standing hours before a mirror trying to comb a few sparse hairs over the top of your head, just throw on an Eva Gabor wig and go on your merry way!

I'll never say never again again

April 15, 1976

Remember the old song, "I'll Never Say Never Again Again?" That should be the parental theme song. When you had no children, or one tiny baby, it was so easy to say exactly what you would never do, or how you'd never be, or what your child would never do. All you needed to do was live long enough to see your kids do exactly whatever it was you said no kid of yours would ever do!

In my hometown of Washington, Iowa, there were three things that you simply didn't do unless nobody cared about you. Two of them were getting your ears pierced and riding on a motorcycle. In the good old days I thought that being struck by lightning would be preferable to doing either of those things. Five years ago my husband, Rick, bought a 750 Honda, and we had a lot of fun on it for more than three years, until we sold it one fall to buy storm windows. Three weeks ago Friday I went to Glenwood and had my fifty-eight-year-old earlobes pierced clear through from front to back. Before doing that, I had the largest collection of clip-on earrings—one of each pair— that has ever been gathered together. I've been promised that we with pierced ears will never lose an earring, and I'm looking forward to that certainty.

The third no-no in Washington, Iowa, used to be that nobody who was anybody had themselves tattooed. At the rate I've been kicking over the former no-no's, I'll probably have an eagle tattooed on my back for the Bicentennial!

We all dance to a different drummer or, who needs it?

June 3, 1976

Saturday Rick and I ordered a new Harley Davidson golf cart because we've had ours four years and the tires are beginning to look a little thin. Get that! With real necessities like golf carts, one can't even wait until they get sick or slow or noisy.

At the other extreme is my ten-year-old vacuum sweeper. For at least six months I've been playing the game of sweep and leak dust balls, bend and pick up with bony fingers, then try sweeping some more. A few things do jump obediently into the hopper, but lint, hair, papers, and so forth remain glued to the carpet until they are removed by hand. We took that monster to the repairman on Saturday, and one hour and ten dollars later the same sweeper became the miracle worker!

Next we outfitted Rick with some new golf clothes (more like what the modern golfers wear). We didn't realize that his golfing outfits were so colorless until we watched a golf match on color TV in the home of friends. On our black-and-white TV sets Rick always looked as colorfully dressed as the golfers!

Speaking of color TV— a person has to have an unlimited amount of self-confidence to admit, in this day and age, to not possessing a color set. Carolyn Owen called me a couple of Saturdays ago and asked me what I was doing. I told her I was watching the baseball game.

She asked, "Aren't the umpires' outfits colorful?"

I replied, "They must be, because I just heard the announcer say the umpires could join the Radio City Rockettes with their colorful outfits."

"You don't see them?" Carolyn questioned me.

"I see them," I said, "but all of the umpires' uniforms are black and white on our set."

"Where on earth *are* you?" she asked.

"It wouldn't matter *where* I was," was my response, "because we don't have a color set anywhere."

"What happened to it?"

"We've never had one," I said. "I didn't know I had to have one. I thought they were mostly for bars and hospitals and

married college students going to college on their parents'
dole."

With that remark, Carolyn diplomatically changed the
subject. I'm hoping she decided we are more to be pitied than
censured!

Happiness is a habit and that's the truth
June 10, 1976

If there were just one thing I could give to a youngster that
would greatly benefit the child throughout life, it would be the
happiness habit. And happiness *is* a habit. It has very little
to do with material things, with the state of health, or with
life's opportunities. It's not what happens to a person in this
life that's important but, rather, how one copes with the
things that happen. Think about it, and people will come to
mind who've had very hard knocks in their lives but are still
smiling and friendly.

On the other hand, you can think of people whose
greatest joy comes from borrowing troubles if there are no
real ones at hand. They can't enjoy a nice rain for fear it might
cause a flood. They can't enjoy a month of sunshine for fear
of a drought. They can't enjoy the prospect of a nice trip for
themselves or loved ones for fear of meeting with an accident
or becoming ill.

- Some of the things people worry about the most never
  happen.
- It's easier on the facial muscles to laugh and smile than
  to frown and cry. And, as the saying goes, "Laugh and
  the world laughs with you; weep and you weep alone."
- Selfishness and unhappiness go hand in hand. The unselfish are too considerate of other people's feelings to
  show a depressed attitude to others.
- Happy people don't feel sorry for themselves, and they
  keep their troubles to themselves rather than try to bur-
  den the world with them.
- Everyone has had some troubles and some times that

have been real tests of their faith and their character, but dwelling on the negative is a waste of time, energy, sleep, and the feeling of well-being. There is no point in going over and over an unfortunate or unpleasant happening. A catchy song was written about accentuating the positive, eliminating the negative, and latching on to "Mr. In-Between."

•Another old saying worthy of mention is, "Don't cry over spilled milk." It's silly to go into a rage when a dish or a vase has been broken or after a car has been wrecked. Nobody is pleased over these happenings, but ranting and raving and screaming after a deed is done can't change it.

Like the happiness habit, self-control can be learned. "I have a terrible temper" is no excuse. I think that is real cause for pity.

As people get older, I've heard it said, they don't change but just get more so of whatever they were before. So I suppose sillier, happier, and more forgetful will be my lot in life. In spite of a few little idiosyncrasies that we all have, you can have the happiness habit if you work at it a bit.Try it—you'll like it!

A slight misunderstanding

February 17, 1977

In reading the "Iowa Farming" section of the *Des Moines Register* this week, I noticed that a certain Lucio Chapa has invented a mechanical corn detasseler. This reminded me of an interesting bit of misinformation that was afloat in our family for one brief week about eighteen years ago.

When our son Courtney was fifteen years old, his grandfather wrote to him in Denver, Colorado, from Washington, Iowa, and told him that he had a summer job detasseling corn. My father, a doctor, had the notoriously illegible handwriting that most doctors seem to have, and in his handwriting the letter read that Courtney could come to Iowa to detassel *cows*.

All of our son's friends and our neighbors thought that Courtney was going to Iowa for the bloody job of cutting tails off cows! It wasn't until he got to Iowa that Courtney discovered the true nature of the job.

Steady are the woman's feet
that trod the streets in men's work shoes
February 24, 1977

When I first came to Malvern, I met a lady in her seventies who was most attractive. She dressed becomingly, with well-chosen jewelry, was vivacious and intelligent, and had lovely hair. Everything about this woman was tasteful and coordinated—unless one happened to glance down at her feet. She wore long, narrow, black oxfords that detracted from her overall appearance. I made a mental resolution that no matter how old I would live to be or how tired my feet would become, I would never stop wearing attractive shoes.

Five years ago Rick gave me some men's work shoes, complete with hooks and rawhide laces. I had been taking four-mile walks in the country in low tennies, and Rick thought I would enjoy some substantial walking shoes. Those work shoes have grown on me. Each year I have worn them more and more, and this winter, with its severe cold, snow, and ice, I took to wearing them for my daily early morning walk to the post office. As the snow and ice continued, my desire to be surefooted increased. First I tried wearing my high-top men's shoes to bridge parties, and when no doors were slammed in my face, I went on from there.

After noticing that I was wearing my super work shoes to dinner with him in Omaha, Rick suggested one Saturday that if I were wearing them "for dress" this winter, they should be polished. He had me take them off, and he polished them nicely. This really encouraged me. After that polish job I wore them to church twice and once to a funeral.

I've worn other, dressier shoes only once this entire month. Marjorie Dashner and I spent Tuesday at Regency Square in Omaha. As I left our house, I grabbed some nice-looking shoes (but flimsy and with slick soles), and I took them with me. But I didn't have any real intentions of changing out of my comfortable work shoes until Marjorie made one little remark. She checked the parking lot carefully, then said, "The parking lot is perfectly dry."

I got the point. She preferred to enter the Sidewalk Cafe with a woman in women's shoes.

If people don't think my winter shoes look nice, I can only hope for an unusually early spring. I still feel that unbroken limbs are beautiful— even mine!

California, here they come

April 21, 1977

This week our daughter Kiffaney and her husband Roger are flying from Denver to San Francisco for a long weekend. Casual observers on the plane might mistake them for spring-vacationing college students, even though they're pushing thirty. In thinking about their wonderful upcoming weekend, I keep going back in my mind to their courtship and marriage and the real struggles they endured in their determination for Roger to get a college education while encumbered with a wife and three children.

Sociologists, psychologists, and other writers have suggested that one of the things causing the breakup of homes and the high number of divorces in our country is that people do not stay in the localities where they were born and reared. Hence they marry persons from different backgrounds and without an opportunity to know members of each other's families before marriage.

Part of this generation's complaint against "The Establishment" was the tendency of parents in the past to judge persons more by the homes from which they came than by what the individual had become. Kiffaney and Roger met in Denver, and neither had met another member of each other's family until they were enroute to be married. Roger was an airman in the air force, and Kiffaney had a summer job as a long-distance operator with the telephone company.

When Kiffaney visited us in Glenwood, we heard a lot about Roger— how wonderful, smart, and considerate he was.

When we asked her by phone the next week if Roger liked the new clothes we had bought her, she said, "I've worn only one new skirt with him because he has only one pair of pants and one pair of shoes, and I don't want him to feel poorly dressed." So I believe we can assume that neither was attracted solely by the other's clothes.

When they decided they wanted to be married, there was a problem. Roger was just nineteen and only two states in the United States (South Carolina and Michigan) allowed a nineteen-year-old boy to be legally married without parental consent. Roger felt sure that his parents wouldn't give consent— they'd think he'd become lonely in the service and had picked up with who knew what— so Roger and Kiffaney decided to go to Michigan and be married. They stopped at our house north of Glenwood overnight, then spent the next night with my mom in Washington, Iowa. Both were asleep on the steps of a courthouse in Michigan when it opened for business on Monday morning.

Their plan, before marriage, was for Roger to finish his stint in the air force, then go back to college for a degree in electric and electronic engineering. They would postpone having a family until Roger was through school. Nine months and five days after they were married, they had a bouncing baby boy, and less than two years later (six weeks before Roger was due to be separated from the air force), they had identical twin boys. By this time Roger was a technical sergeant, and they wondered if he should give up that much security and try to get through college with five mouths to feed. But leave they did. They were stationed in Limestone, Maine, when Roger left the service. He wanted to take his engineering degree at Oregon State University, so they stopped here on their way to Oregon— all five of them in a Volkswagen Beetle that hadn't self-started since they left Maine; they had to push it to start it.

One thing I remember about that visit was a statement our son-in-law made that endeared him to me more than ever. We all had been invited to Lorance Lisle's beautiful farm home near Hastings for a Sunday buffet dinner, and Rick was going to ride his motorcycle. He invited Roger to ride with him, but Roger (twenty-one or twenty-two at the time) said he didn't want to do that because he had too many responsibilities. So Granny and Grandpa rode the motorcycle out there and back, and the young folks followed in our Toronado. That was one of the first times I got the feeling that I've had so many times since: Grannies have more fun.

I could write a book about the young couple's experiences in getting Roger through college, beginning with the VW completely conking out seventy-five miles from Denver and their having to hitchhike into Denver with three babes in arms. I would continue through those first years when Kiffaney did bookkeeping in a medical clinic at nights alone in a spooky building. She ushered in a theater, and Roger stocked grocery shelves, and they did anything else they could find to do. The last two years went better because Roger got a job working forty hours a week for the oceanography department at the university, making computers and instruments for shipboard experiments.

Roger made Eta Kappa Nu honorary society for engineers and graduated with highest honors in a suit from the Goodwill store. Now he's new product director/coordinator of engineering for International Medical Corporation in Denver, working with microcomputers and designing medical equipment.

Kiffaney and Roger Frank have one of the most loving marriages I've ever witnessed, and I'm glad that I never gave them any sweat about being too young or not well enough acquainted or not well enough educated to get married.

Our sleeping porch

May 10, 1977

You can't imagine what you've missed if you've never slept on a sleeping porch. Our sleeping porch, like every other part of our property, is surrounded by trees. Songbirds are our alarm clocks. From our lofty bed we can view the cattle pastured at Ted Bowen's and Jim Beattie's. It's nice starting each new day with that top-of-the-world feeling. Screened windows on three sides give a "great outdoors" atmosphere without mosquitoes and flies biting and buzzing.

*After sleeping on a sleeping porch, morning finds one rested
    and wiser
The good fresh air that hits us there acts as a tranquilizer!
Our houseguests I always try to please, but this I must confide
If you visit us in the summertime, you'll have to sleep inside!*

A couple of long-disturbance worries
March 16, 1978

Our son Courtney hadn't taken time to see a dentist for years. In our last letter from his wife, Suzie, she wrote that Courtney had been to the dentist for two sessions and had yet another appointment to have his teeth cleaned. I felt as if I'd had a weight lifted and was temporarily in seventh heaven—until Suzie penned, "Now my next goal is to have him get a driver's license. He hasn't had one since we left Chicago six years ago."

That's the kind of news that shouldn't ever be told to a silver-wigged mother. I really felt frantic. Here's this guy hauling prospective homebuyers all over southeast Denver in that God-awful traffic, and he isn't even licensed to drive! Had he been in an accident, they could have thrown the book at him, to say nothing of all the lawsuits that could have come from injuries to passengers. Of course, he has a phone in his car (maybe a TV and a bathroom, too?) but no driver's license.

I try not to horn into my kids' business (one of the obvious reasons being that they do as they please anyway), but I did write Courtney a letter and told him that all I wanted for my birthday was a copy of his legal driving license. He went and got one, and I'm walking on air again. They didn't even give him a bad time about it or ask him where he'd been the last six years. They didn't bat an eye when he gave them an expired Hinsdale, Illinois, license. Maybe my conscience

The sleeping porch

bothered me a little in the "setting a good example" department because I had my driver's license suspended for six
months when Courtney was a teenager.

What are best friends for?

September 21, 1978

I love people and find it difficult to draw the line when I'm
entertaining. Not only that, but I can't count too well. The second year that I lived in Glenwood, after I had become acquainted with the bridge players, I used to give bridge parties
to which I'd invite one or two too many players. I could always
sit out myself (which I hate doing), but there'd still be too
many players.

The first time I overinvited, by one person, I called Ardeth
McLaughlin and asked, "Would you like to be known as my
best friend?" She sounded a little reluctant but finally agreed
to the title. Then I told her that she'd either have to sit out at
her house or at my house. Ardeth put up with this about three
times. She couldn't have been sweeter about it.

Then I moved to Malvern, and at my first bridge party the
number of invitees was not divisible by four. What to do! I
called Marilyn Burdic (whom I'd talked to about three times)
and asked, "Would you like the honor of being known as my
best friend?" The tone of her voice indicated that she thought
I was a real dingbat, but she agreed to sit out and pretend that
she hadn't come to play but just to make friends.

Eventually I learned to count better and didn't need
friends to even up numbers after a while, but this last spring
and summer I've needed best friends for another reason. The
dry-cleaning service to Malvern was suddenly cut off, so I
leaned on the Glenwood bridge club girls again to be my best
friends and pick up our cleaning and bring it to bridge club
for me. Ardeth McLaughlin, Betty Bales, Jo Campbell, and
Carol Dean have done a land office business for us at Ring's
Cleaners.

They groan at bridge club when I start the best friend
routine, but who would ask an *enemy* to fetch and carry?

Five often-heard quotes that don't pertain to me
November 16, 1978

1. "Why don't you take time to eat?" Eating doesn't take time. I can eat the equivalent of a Thanksgiving dinner while hanging over the kitchen sink clearing the dinner dishes.
2. "She should let up a little and stop working so hard." I've always managed to sandwich-in rest and relaxation at the drop of a hat.
3. "Her floors are so clean that you could eat off of them." Who needs to eat from the floor when there are tables in every room?
4. "She never takes time to smell the flowers." I've smelled and smelled and smelled the flowers while the other housewives were doing the mundanes of endlessly vacuuming and dusting.
5. "Everything goes for the house and nothing for herself." If there were a showdown between buying a hinge to keep the front door on and something important like new shaggy, flirty, false eyelashes, I'd opt for the lashes any day!

Proving the horoscopes to be wrong
March 15, 1979

Rick and I really don't put much faith in horoscopes, but we do read them often and laugh about them. Last night both of ours said that Sunday we might have a disagreement with our loved one. You've never seen two more agreeable people than we were today.

I can't remember any specific wonderful things I've done today, but Rick agreed instantly on two things that he sometimes balks at. When I saw how beautiful it was outside, I suggested a long walk in the country—at least four miles. Rick said fine, and we went.

Then I thought it would be the perfect time to ask if Rick would like to go to the Glen Haven auxiliary bridge benefit in Glenwood the next night. Many times he tells me that he'd really appreciate my going with a friend instead, but today he

said he'd go if I really wanted him to. I do! I do!
Help cometh from the strangest places.

Fool's paradise, or pinch me to prove I'm awake, or old folks need guardians
May 3, 1979

From 1950 to 1967 I drove and loved convertibles. In 1968 I ordered a hugger orange Sting Ray convertible from the Jim Stanley Chevrolet dealership in Glenwood. That was the one year they were in short supply. Jim was a new dealer and wasn't able to get me one.

I tried to tell myself that I didn't care, but every time I've seen a convertible during the past twelve years, I've had goose bumps, heavy breathing, and other unhealthy symptoms. When most companies stopped making ragtops, I expected a return to normalcy. No such luck!

Rick is as bananas over Oldsmobile Toronados (front-wheel drive) as I am over convertibles. He's had two of them. Not only does he like the way they perform, but he loves their spaciousness, comfort, and tilt steering wheel, which allows him to get in with ease. Oldsmobile had never made a Toronado convertible. So imagine our surprise and ecstasy to see a bright red Toronado convertible at the Oldsmobile dealership in Omaha recently. This had to be some kind of omen. The dealer had bought it from a man in Lima, Ohio, who had customized it from a sedan. It had only the 1,100 miles that it takes to drive from Ohio to Omaha. We asked for a quote on the rock-bottom price, then went home to brood. Sunday we decided it was out of the question, but Monday I wrote the following letter:

Dear Sirs:

Saturday night my husband and I both fell in love with your red Toro convertible. My husband has had two Toros in the past and liked them very much. I've wanted a Sting Ray convertible for over twelve years. We're retirement age, and I think we could make a great compromise on a Toro convertible. Wouldn't that be a cute old folks' last car?

We are prepared to offer you cash with no trade-in cars. (I then subtracted enough for the sales tax and one year's insurance from the price quoted us.)

We're scared to trade in our gas-saving Mazda or VW in view of the fact that we might not be able to get enough gas to run the red beauty farther than in downtown Malvern.

We'll be happy any way you decide on this matter. We both would be very excited about getting this car but have scary thoughts about paying so much for one just because we like it and not because it's necessary for transportation.

Most sincerely,
GRANNY SMITH

Then I enclosed a picture of myself. (Doesn't everyone, when dealing for a car?) Our salesman called me Tuesday to say they'd accept our offer. He said the boss's daughter had

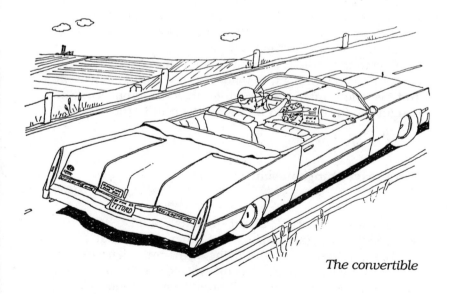

The convertible

opened the letter and said, "I don't care what we have in it. Let them have it for their price."

Rick said, "They know a live one when they see one."

I think "live one" means the same as "sucker."

Tuesday we went up and made a deposit on the car and were to pick it up Thursday evening. Tuesday night I didn't close an eye. I had more misgivings than Rexall has pills! I told Rick we'd made a mistake, and he agreed with me. He appointed me as a committee of one to call the salesman. So I called Mr. Cram and told him that we had nowhere to keep the car, couldn't afford the gas for it, and on and on. This phone call gave me great relief. I was happy we had come to our senses.

Saturday we were on our way to Shenandoah in the Mazda to meet friends for lunch. Four miles down Highway 34 Rick said, "I hate these darned little cars. I can't even turn in this seat."

"I know where there's a beautiful, comfortable car," I responded.

When we arrived at the Oldsmobile place after lunch, our salesman didn't even change expressions. He hadn't torn up the bill of sale or sent back our deposit. He knew we'd be back. We'll enjoy the car until we won't be permitted to drive anymore. Then we can park it in the front yard and admire it from our rocking chairs on the front porch.

Our compromise on the car reminds me of one that Henny Youngman and his wife made. Henny wanted a new car and his wife wanted a fur coat, so they compromised. She bought the fur coat, and they kept the coat in the garage.

Don't leave things unsaid

June 14, 1979

In reading an article about the crash of a DC 10, I was reminded that plane crashes and other things that cause death sometimes leave the living with much left unsaid. Expressing your feelings to those you love gets easier and easier the more you do it. All your true sentiment-giving shouldn't be left to Hallmark. If you care enough, you should write exactly how you feel yourself. I'd rather have three very personal lines written by a loved one than a book written to me by someone who didn't know me. It's possible to pick up a card in a store, address it, and mail it without thinking more than three minutes about the person who is to receive it.

Some of my more precious belongings are notes, cards, and letters from our children, telling why we are special to them. Some of these I've even put in the lockbox at the bank, because that's how I rate them as objects too rare to chance losing.

Our family is into the third generation of expressing love for one another in this way, and the grandchildren have never sent us anything but handmade cards. When we come for a visit, they also make cards expressing their pleasure. Taped to the refrigerator door is a card that Tyler gave Grandpa the last time we visited them:

Dear Grandpa,

> I'm so glad you came. I hope you have fun with us.
> Nice seeing someone as speshal as you again!

> > > > > Love,
> > > > > TYLER FRANK

Finally, he drew a heart and wrote "I love you" inside the heart.

While I'm on the subject of family living and loving, I hope you remember to be as kind and polite to the children in your family as you are to strangers.

Just because children are young and haven't lived long enough to know everything, it doesn't mean they want to be corrected and talked down to every time they enter a room. Children blossom from praise like anyone else, and a child who's told how nice he or she is often enough is much more apt to be that way than one who's told to "stick in your shirttail," "stand up straight," "quit acting stupid," or "get lost," every time he or she puts in an appearance.

Thanks to the horse chasers

October 2, 1980

You know you live in a small town when six people take the time to try to corral your horses that somehow manage to get out only when you're out of town. We're really grateful to Andy Click, Rex Adair, Tom Gidley, Dee Hatfield, Mary Click, and Dottie Graham.

I understand that it was a cool day and Rick's horses (Prince, Silver, and Hobo) were feeling very frisky. When our friends' chasing them brought no results, Tom thought that if Mary would go to our house and drive Rick's old red 1966 Dodge pickup truck down there, the horses would think Rick was driving and would run up to the truck. But this caused them to hesitate only slightly, and when Mary, rather than the master, alighted from the truck, they kicked up their heels and were off again. I don't know if the horses just ran out of steam or whether our friends outsmarted them, but the horses were safely returned to their pasture eventually.

We were told that our own blonde, very feminine co-editor of the *Malvern Leader*, Dottie, was the first to get ahold of one of the horses. From then on, Dee, who has horses at home, knew the next steps to take. It would have made a good home movie scenario!

If you love them, tell them so!

December 11, 1980

How long has it been since you've told your parents how much you think of them or how much they mean to you? Kiffaney wrote this week, "We are all so excited about our Christmas visit to Iowa, and the Firehouse Dinner Theater of *Oklahoma* sounds great. The boys are feeling very grown up to be included in that outing.

"I miss you so badly sometimes I don't think I can stand it . . . then I feel just lucky to have parents that arouse such a warm feeling. I worry sometimes that you don't know how wonderful you are to all of us and that you may think that all of your efforts are really not appreciated. Sometimes the message is missed with the people you love the very most . . ."

The above sentiments had Rick and me walking on air for hours. Most people do love and admire their parents and feel warm toward them, but they just assume that their parents know this without their saying it. Don't say it if you don't mean it, but if you do have something nice to say to your parents, for heaven's sakes spit it out!

They can have it—if there's some left
November 3, 1981

I have never understood the middle-aged people whose main aim in life is to leave lots of money for their children when they depart this world. They don't travel places they'd enjoy going. They don't buy new clothes. They don't redecorate their homes or entertain company. My parents felt that the most important things you could give your children were a college education and a faith in the Lord. I'd add to that a sense of humor.

It seems to me that if you rear stupid kids, someone will dupe them out of any money you leave them anyway. If you rear smart kids, they can earn their own money.

We saw the cutest bumper sticker recently on a very expensive, elegant car that an elderly couple drove down the highway: "We're spending our children's inheritance."

Let's keep the hens employed
January 15, 1983

I get cross with recipe-givers who would have a body believe that you can have a gorgeous meringue on your soft pies using just two egg whites. For a really high meringue it takes more like four, five, six, eight, or ten (who's counting?). Pull the drapes, lock the doors, take the phone off the hook, and beat up as many egg whites as you like. It isn't wasteful either, if you want a gorgeous looking pie for a special occasion, as there are many ways to use up all those egg yolks, in everything from scrambled eggs to pancakes, in escalloped corn, and for French toast.

For the people who have viewed my meringue pies as unusual and impossible to match, I can only say that they have been too saving of egg whites. Live dangerously— use a whole bunch of egg whites!

On calling each spouse by the correct name
May 31, 1983

Sunday we were up early and went to both cemeteries (Malvern and Glenwood) to decorate the graves of former spouses. This is the season of the year, if we're going to, that we occasionally have a slip of the tongue and sometimes I call Rick "Courtney" and Rick calls me "Gretchen."

I excuse myself by thinking that when an elderly lady has had a very happy twenty-six years of marriage with one nice person before she's into an equally happy marriage for fourteen years with another dreamy man, it's only natural that she'd mix them up. Isn't it? Wouldn't you?

Once when Rick had a caller in the living room, I came downstairs all dressed up and Rick explained to the guest that "Gretchen's going to Glenwood to play bridge tonight."

I said, "Good. Maybe we can ride over together, because that's where I'm going, too."

One morning I knocked on Rick's bathroom door and asked, "Courtney, do you want oatmeal for breakfast?"

Rick answered, "I don't know about Courtney, but I'd like some."

Later, while we were eating breakfast, I said, "After all, I have a son by the name of Courtney, too."

Rick's reply was, "That may be, but I know who you planned to feed that oatmeal to."

Praise for the Glenwood Library luncheon speaker-to-be

April 23, 1983

Judy Delashmutt called and asked if I would give the Glenwood Friends of the Library luncheon a plug in my column. I asked what the program was to be, and she asked, "Do you know who Joan Burney is?"

"Do I know who she is? I've only idolized her for about four years and never dreamed I'd get to meet her in person."

Four years ago I had spoken at the Beta Sigma Phi mother-daughter banquet at the Sundowner Club in Glenwood. A lady called me the next day and asked me to speak at the Omaha Catholic Daughters of America Christmas banquet at the Peony Park ballroom. She said they'd like the same type of speech I had given at the sorority banquet on the topic of "Grannies Have More Fun," when I had elaborated on one of my favorite topics— the one declaring happiness as a habit and losing your enthusiasm for living wrinkles your soul.

At this huge Christmas banquet at Peony Park, I was seated between Father Frank Partusch and Archbishop Daniel Sheehan (and I'm not even a Catholic). After I finished speaking, the Archbishop complimented me on my speech, then said, "Your philosophy of life is similar to a friend of mine who lives in Hartington, Nebraska. Her name is Joan Burney, and she also writes a column for a weekly newspaper."

I was curious and sent in money for a subscription to the *Cedar County News*. From reading her columns, I learned that she's a happy, helpful, loving, and well-adjusted person. She loves people, hasn't a jealous or malicious bone in her body, and can really laugh at herself. Sometimes Joan Burney says she's promoting wrinkles. She pokes fun at this country's pursuit of everlasting youth. She suggests accepting middle age and the wrinkles that go with it. After all, she says, "We look pleasant; we look interesting, mature, and trustworthy." Mrs. Burney believes that people have to be able to laugh at themselves: "It is not only desirable— it's a necessity!"

Frederick G. Smith has a birthday

May 31, 1985

The neatest person I know— the kindest, most considerate, most genteel, lovable man in the world— will be seventy years old today. Every day I love Rick more! He's such fun, so enthusiastic and energetic, that I can't understand why as a young girl I thought anyone over sixty must be blah and boring. Rick is tireless and clever about any household, yard, or garden project that he undertakes. At the same time, he doesn't expect others (specifically, me) to work full tilt at all times. Rick is easy to please and appreciative of my cooking and baking.

I trust Rick and feel free to tell him everything I see, hear, and think. He lets me make my own plans and decisions, but he sometimes tells me if he thinks he has a better idea. Then I'm free to take it or leave it.

Rick is great company, whether down at the Three Horse Ranch or by ourselves for twenty-four hours or in a crowd. Rick makes me feel good about myself just by the way he looks at me. I know that mirrors don't lie, but I feel like a young girl when I'm with Rick.

When I stop and think how loyal and kind Rick is to his horses, Silver, Prince, and Hobo, it reinforces how secure I feel about him. The loving care those horses get in their old age— the money, the work, the sacrifices he makes for them! Surely, if he's that good to them, he's not likely to ever kick out his old lady.

A mud bath!

October 17, 1985

Rick had a new experience on Friday. We were golfing in a husband-wife tourney at Glenwood, and I lost a ball on the number four hole by Keg Creek. But I first should explain that I refuse to look for golf balls because in his den Rick has egg cartons full of them stacked from the floor up about eight shelves. We have enough for both our lifetimes, unless we attain a new record for longevity. To Rick, each golf ball is a precious thing to be treasured and appreciated, and to which he clings with every breath.

Anyway, he started down a rough creek bank to retrieve my ball, and he lost his footing. The water was the muddiest I'd ever seen it. Rick landed on his back in the mud, wedged between the two sides of the narrow creek so he couldn't even move. There he lay with muddy water filling his ears, but he was holding up the arm on which he wears his watch, pipe still in mouth, and glasses not even awry on his face. One of our golf partners, Leonard Schuster, leaned down and practically had to pull Rick out of that mud hole. If you've seen mud wrestling on TV, you can imagine what Rick looked like. He wasn't even fit to ride back to the clubhouse in our golf cart. He lined the seat of his pickup with towels and hurried back to Malvern to shower and change clothes.

When we played golf in Missouri Valley yesterday, Tom Davis declared that he had brought some waterwings in case Rick might lose a ball up there somewhere!

Our daughter is . . .

October 30, 1985

Our daughter is

. . . someone who lives 600 miles away, yet manages to see us at least every other month.

. . . someone who anticipates when we could use a phone call, letter, or card— and always comes through.

. . . someone who knows all of our idiosyncrasies and faults but still wouldn't trade us for any other parents she knows.

. . . someone we thought was too tough on her sons and made them grow up too fast— but we like the results.

. . . someone who's so well-adjusted and pleased with herself that she's secure enough to be happy with the people and the world around her.

. . . someone who lives by the golden rule. She puts

herself in the place of others, then treats them as she would like to be treated.

. . . someone who knows what she thinks on every subject. She's not wishy-washy and doesn't change her opinions to coincide with those of whomever she's speaking. She doesn't care how the majority feels about the new morality. She thinks it's for the birds.

. . . this world's most appreciative person. She tells her husband, children, friends, and parents often how important they are to her.

. . . thirty-nine years old today and looks twenty-five. She's happy, bubbly, laughing, and eager for each new day.

. . . someone who isn't nice enough to let her bewigged old mother beat her at bridge. (Kiffaney, couldn't you let down once and throw a game to me?)

What does a mother know?

January 9, 1986

Sunday morning Kiffaney called from Littleton, Colorado, asking, "Do you want to hear the latest news about a relative of yours that hit the *Denver Post* this morning?" I have fifteen relatives in Denver and was wondering if one of them had contracted AIDS, cheated on income taxes, or robbed a bank to buy my Christmas present. It was none of the above. Kiffaney said that Courtney, our son, was pictured with another man, along with an article telling about their being the top two realtors in Denver. Courtney had been asked to what he attributed his success, and he didn't say, "All that I am or ever hope to be I owe to my angel mother." Instead he said, "I have a big ego, and I always have to be in the top twenty."

The more I thought about it, the more I knew that I didn't deserve any credit, because my advice to him fourteen years ago was to stay with Sears and be secure for life. Courtney's second job out of college was with Sears in Denver. Within two years he was selected to go into the main office in Chicago. He and his family hated Chicago, and in less than a year's time, he quit his job, rented a U-Haul, and headed back to Colorado. I was absolutely sick about it because of Sears' pension and stock-buying options.

They had lived in an apartment in Chicago, and when they stopped to visit us en route back to Denver, our granddaughter Ashley (four at the time) said, "Grandma, we got out of our cage." As they pulled out, I said to Rick, "Everyone wants to live in Colorado, so they'll work for less there. He'll never have as good a job as he had with Sears."

The first week back in Denver, Courtney landed a job as a buyer for the ski department at the May Company. He wrote us a long letter relating the many advantages and benefits connected with working for the May Company.

About a month later, when Peg Buffington and I went to Denver for a bridge retreat, we stayed with Suzie and Court-ney. The first night there, Courtney said, "Sit down, Mom, I want to tell you something." Then he told me he was going to sell real estate. I nearly had cardiac arrest.

So what does a mother know? No wonder children be-come deaf when their parents start advising them!

Grandchildren

Sunday afternoon at Boehner's Pond

May 27, 1976

Ever since the first week he came, our visiting eight-year-old grandson Bradley had been trying to promote a fishing trip. Last Friday Grandpa Rick bought him a new rod and reel and started teaching him how to cast— in the front yard. It had rained during the night, so it was easy to find fish worms.

On Sunday, with enough supplies to stake us for a week in Canada, we headed for Boehner's Pond, less than a half mile from our back door. We set up housekeeping on two folding chairs and a camp stool on the banks of the pond. The red-winged blackbirds supplied the music, and an occasional tree toad chimed into the chorus.

Bradley was the first to catch a fish— a ten-inch bullhead— and such a thrill it was for him! Grandpa showed him how to put it on a stringer and keep it in the water. We sat there for four-and-one-half hours chock full of optimism, enjoying the beauty of the spot and the good air. The only other catch was a small bluegill that was too small and had to be thrown back for next year.

Upon arriving home with our lone fish, the misunderstanding began. Bradley didn't want his fish killed. He wanted to keep it. When Grandpa said we had nothing bigger than a bucket to keep it in, Bradley rejoined, "It seems to me that some people don't think very much before they go fishing."

"What do you mean?" Grandpa asked.

"I mean you shouldn't go and catch fish if you don't have any place nicer than a bucket to keep them in," Bradley retorted.

I really thought I was dreaming when I saw Grandpa go to the garage and get out the kiddie swimming pool and fill it with water for that bullhead.

During dinner we had quite a discussion about catching, killing, and eating fish. We said perhaps Bradley didn't like fishing and we shouldn't go again. Bradley said that he liked fishing fine but he couldn't understand killing his fish when it was such a nice fish. Then, he told Grandpa, when the fish died by itself, we could eat it if we wanted to. We said we didn't want to do that. Before the meal was over, it had been decided to return the nice fish to the pond from whence it came. And that's a wonderful thing about fishing near home— it doesn't take an hour or more of your time to return the fish!

The moral to this story is: If you're a fish, be a nice fish!

Ashley and Kristy visit Malvern

July 8, 1976

Our two darling granddaughters arrived from Denver on Thursday. They corrected me concerning their ages, and we raved about how grown up they are for their years. Ashley will be eight for two more months, and little sister Kristy is four.

I had a very important bridge club on the first night they came, which Rick said he'd try to explain to them. He took them down to take care of his horses, out to the country to see some baby pigs and kittens, to the park to see the new barrel ride, and to the front porch for firefly hunting.

Friday night Ashley was busy writing something and making a book while we were reading the newspapers. The next morning when we came to the breakfast table, the book was sitting at Grandpa's place. It was entitled *"Music I Rote"* by Ashley Kline. The inside title was "Horses," followed by the words to her song:

How I love horses, horses, horses,
when ever I see them I try to get on one.
I JUST CAN'T STAND IT
i want to ride a horse all over the world.
I would like to have one: we live where you can't have them.
So I just ride them in Iowa, Iowa, Iowa.

Rick and I don't have to have a building fall on us to catch a hint. The girls had been here one and one-half days, and nobody had mentioned their riding Grandpa's horses. Ashley felt it was high time something was done about it. We put that on the agenda for the first thing the morning of the Fourth of July. In the afternoon, while Grandpa was getting in his twenty-seven holes of golf, Dorothea Thomas and the girls and I went to the ice cream social on the lawn of the old General Dodge House in Council Bluffs. That was like turning back the pages of time a couple hundred years. Old cars were parked out in front, a barbershop quartet provided entertainment, the beautiful old fountain had been turned on, and people sat around and ate ice cream and cake and drank lemonade. Dorothea wore a long, linen, horseless carriage coat and bonnet, and I tried to look the part in a long gray flowered dress trimmed in black velvet.

A picnic that evening at the John Deans' country home near Glenwood put the perfect touch on our Fourth of July. Three other families were there, plus two of Jeff Dean's buddies from the University of Wyoming. Eleven-year-old Grant Dean let Ashley and Kristy take turns on his trampoline and showed them all of his pets. Besides their regular handsome horses, the Deans have a beautiful new thoroughbred seven-year-old horse in the barn. They also have a peacock and a peahen, a hamster, and three well-trained Rottweiler dogs.

After a sumptuous meal we had a huge volleyball game. One of Jeff's friends from Wyoming, who is on the football team, boosted our team, but Bill Campbell, superintendent of the state hospital school, was on the other team and kept calling out the scores— not accurately but loudly! We played that game way past dark. Then Jeff and his friends put on a fireworks display for us.

It's really wonderful when a party with an age range of

four to sixty-one can be such fun! And our two little grand-daughters were made to feel that the party had been planned around them.

The beetle boys

August 3, 1976

Our son Courtney related this story about his sister Kiffaney, her husband, and their three sons. It seems that they wanted to go to a drive-in movie but thought a Volkswagen beetle would offer too much togetherness for a family of five for four hours. So they took both of their VW beetles.

When they arrived at the drive-in theater, Kiffaney got out of hers, leaving the three boys in the front seat and joining her husband Roger in his VW.

What would you think if you were to park at a drive-in, glance at the next car, and see it occupied solely by three young boys (one eight-year-old and six-year-old twins)? Courtney and his wife Suzie, who are blessed with two lady-like girls, couldn't imagine wanting to be in a different car from their children!

And Kiffaney has several other sly little tricks up her sleeve for summertime retreats. When they're at the swimming pool and she sees antics of her sons that displease her, she swims 20 laps or— if it's really grim— dives in and sits at the bottom of the pool. Now I see how she keeps her cool! It beats counting to ten because it lasts longer and gives her more time to consider what course of action to take.

Granny or the 7-Up?

March 2, 1977

Our daughter had asked us to refrain from giving their sons soda pop. We *tried* to follow orders. I gave seven-year-old Tyler about two tablespoons of 7-Up in a juice glass and headed for the front porch with the rest of the bottle. Tyler asked, "Grandma, are you going to drink all the rest of that yourself?"

I replied, "Unless I drop dead."

Then Tyler asked, "Grandma, if you drop dead, can I please pour all the rest in my glass?"

I had the strange feeling that he would gladly trade his dead grandmother for a nearly full bottle of 7-Up!

More 7-up. . .

I don't remember saying that!

November 3, 1977

In 1955, when my mother was sixty-one years old, she wrote this in her diary:

"October 14th— Sorry I have neglected this old book— what a summer! Kiffaney arrived the first week in June and stayed until the 1st of Aug. Robin and Johnnie flew in from Baltimore the last week in June and were here 3-1/2 weeks. Gin Sue and Doug came the last week in June from New York and stayed until the 15th of August. Robert and Helene came with Reed and Peter and that made seven grandchildren and the oldest was eight and the youngest was three.

"We had a wonderful time. They didn't get along as well together as I had hoped but I'm sure they had fun. Daddy took it in his stride and did all he could to help."

This gives you an idea of what kind of grandparents our children had. At the time, I didn't think too much about it, because I didn't know then how rare grandparents like those are. Since I've been a grandmother and our daughter Kiffaney has always made such a point of wanting only one of their boys at a time to visit us, I've thought about it. Kiffaney keeps a systematic account of whose turn it is, and it makes me feel very guilty about the way we always overloaded our parents with grandchildren. It's been a point of pride that I have such a considerate daughter, and I've bragged about it often to anyone who would listen.

When our niece Linda Finlay visited us from Menlo Park, California, this past summer, I told her about how much more considerate Kiffaney was of us than we had been of our parents. When Linda left here, she went to visit Kiffaney. The next time I talked to Kiffaney long distance she said, "Linda said that you told her I wouldn't ever send more than one of my kids at a time to visit you."

I agreed, "Yes, I told her about it."

Kiffaney went on, "There's an excellent reason why I don't."

"What's that?" I asked.

"You told me *never again!* "

"I don't remember saying that," I said, puzzled.

Kiffaney said that when her boys were all babies, I kept

them for three weeks. The first week I wrote to Kiffaney and Roger each day, she said, telling them what a darling family they had and all of the cute things they had been doing. The second week they didn't hear from me at all. The third week, when Kiffaney called, I said (according to her), "I never again want more than one of these kids at a time, unless there's a death in the family— preferably mine!" I would take an oath that I don't recall ever feeling that way or saying that, but it does sound like something I'd say, so I guess I'll have to believe it.

So I said, "That doesn't go anymore anyway. Send them all out tomorrow."

Kiffaney responded, "It's too late now. The pattern's set, and they love being the only child at Grandma and Grandpa's."

Ho hum! I lucked out again!

But Courtney and I don't make our B's backwards
December 15, 1977

This week I was analyzed by an expert, our daughter Kiffaney. Have you ever been told that a picture in a magazine, or a neighbor, or a cousin, reminded someone of you? And how curious you were to see that person, or at least a picture, to glimpse how you appear to others?

There are three boys in Kiffaney's family, a nine-year-old and a pair of seven-year-old twins. Nathan, one of the twins, is the one who needs the most correction and parental guidance. Kiffaney told my sister Virginia that she thought Nathan was more like our son Courtney and Granny. It really puzzled me just how Courtney, Nathan, and I are alike, so I wrote to Kiffaney and asked her. Now I know.

Her reply was: "I didn't really mean anything substantial when I said Nate is more like you and Courtney, as you know I think a lot of both of you— he's just a shade different than Brad and Ty— he falls more readily into the 'good life.' He couldn't understand why on earth we would live in a motel a month while waiting to get in our new home, when it doesn't have a swimming pool. He suggests eating out daily— he doesn't give a hang where his clothes go— unlike my other two sorters. This morning he dumped the sand from his shoes on the floor, then put the MAID REQUESTED sign on the door. When he writes a letter, he doesn't ask anyone how to spell anything, and he still makes his B's backwards sometimes and just assumes that everything will come out all right in the end."

Just what they wanted to hear

February 16, 1978

I have often told our children that the only thing I regret about my whole life, and the only thing I would do differently if I had my life to live over, would be to change from having such a child-centered home as we had. I was one of those dippy mothers who couldn't really enjoy two weeks on the beach at Acapulco with my husband and friends because I'd be thinking about how the little darlings at home would have enjoyed being there.

During the time the children were in junior high and high school (until they were old enough to drive), we never accepted a dinner or party invitation until I had first checked with the children to make sure they didn't need a ride to a party or a school activity. I never donned a pair of skis, but we spent more money sending the kids up to the slopes on the ski train every Saturday, paying for their ski tows, ski lessons, and the rest of it, than we did for groceries. And we thought they had to have the best piano teacher in Denver for five solid years each— but we could have gotten more music out of a nickelodeon.

Our children and their mates are excellent parents, in my view, and I'm especially aware that they listened well, too, when I said from time to time that the children's turn could come later and that parents should not sacrifice so much for their children. Yesterday Kiffaney called me from Vail, Colorado, where she had gone skiing with her friend Judy while Roger and the boys were shifting for themselves for a few days. Tomorrow Rick and I will be picking up Ashley and

Kristy at the airport for a ten-day visit while Suzie and Courtney take a Caribbean cruise.

As our granddaughters stepped off the plane on their last visit, they informed us of the biggest blunders we had made during their previous visit: "Grandma, you're not supposed to cut any bangs on either of us. Our bedtime is nine o'clock, not eleven o'clock, during vacation. And you're not supposed to put any of our jeans or slacks in the dryer."

Who says?

Little girls are fun, too!

August 30, 1979

I had forgotten how much imagination little girls have until Kristy and Ashley came a week ago. They make a wonderful adventure of everything they do.

They put a sign on our dining room door stating, "Please wait to be seated." We do that before dinner every night. Our dining room has been named "Granny's Dinner House." Ashley is the hostess and dinner waitress, and Kristy is the dessert waitress. They print menus every afternoon, and I have to let them know early in the day what the meal will be so they can proceed with the menu.

They have made privacy signs for their bedroom doors. Even the most commonplace happening is a drama for Ashley. For instance, after twisting her ankle while she and Kristy and Tyler were skating, she went upstairs to her bedroom. When I went up there later, the sign outside her door read: "Hurt person inside— if you urgently need to talk to me, knock gently three times." I knocked gently three times, whereupon Ashley invited me in. She was languishing on her bed and asked me not to tell Kristy and Tyler that she wasn't really hurt.

They play school and make notebooks and write themes by the hour. Grandpa and I have graded about forty papers a day. They love wearing my high-heeled boots and my doughnut-hole wooden platform shoes. Sometimes they're teachers and sometimes they're high school girls. And several times they've been dogs, drinking from bowls of water on the floor.

While they've been here, Grandpa has worked two whole days cleaning his den. The back porch is full of throw-away stuff. He now has a sign taped to the side of his desk: "Grandpa has earned this award for attempting to clean his den" (signed, Ashley). I think the glow of winning that award was dulled for Grandpa by the word "attempting."

Dumb dots on the soles yet!

October 12, 1978

We received a letter from Kiffaney giving a blow-by-blow account of their Saturday. Tuesday the winter soccer schedule is to begin, and both Nathan and Tyler needed new soccer shoes. Kiffaney had heard about an outlet store that sells name-brand shoes at half what she'd paid for the previous pairs, so she decided to look into them.

Tyler quickly found some soccer shoes to his liking, but the ones Nathan preferred had some dots— on the soles, mind you— that he just couldn't live with. He said he would rather have none than to get those with dumb dots on the soles. Kiffaney asked him who could see the dots when he was walking or running. Nathan didn't reply. When he ended up in tears, Kiffaney decided that the world wouldn't collapse if Nathan didn't play soccer this season, and they went home.

But his father thought it would be too bad for Nathan not to play, because he'd already paid his fifteen-dollar fee. Roger said he'd take Nathan someplace and buy him any kind of shoes just so the kid's feet were covered. Nathan was also given the choice of taking his own Christmas money to buy the expensive kind that he was used to wearing if he couldn't be happy with some cheaper shoes. This rotten idea brought more tears. Father and son ended up buying some canvas-type soccer shoes for less than half the price of expensive ones, and Nathan stated that he probably would never wear the shoes anywhere!

I can imagine how Kiffaney and Roger felt— they probably

had lumps in their throats and sweaty palms, like parents get when they're trying their darndest and aren't sure it's enough. But the payoff came when Nathan put on the new shoes just before dinner, walked into the kitchen all smiles, and said, "These are kind of neat shoes, Mom. I'm sorry if I caused you some trouble today."

What's in a letter?

December 11, 1980

Almost every week our daughter's letters contain something that strikes us funny about her boys. This week she wrote, "Nathan figured out a unique way to empty the bathroom trash yesterday. He flushed it down the toilet!" She spared us the dirty details of that story.

She told another anecdote about a girl friend's visit to their home. Of Kiffaney's six best girl friends from high school and college, only Linda, besides herself, has any children. These childless friends have visited Kiffaney and Roger in Oregon and in New Mexico, and now two of them have visited in South Carolina. Always before, when one of them came for a visit, Kiffaney would tell her boys exactly how they were to speak and act and what the noise level would be while they had company. But this time, before Edna came, Kiffaney told the boys to just do what they had to do. While reading this, I thought to myself that she was giving them quite a bit of leeway.

Later on the phone I asked Kiffaney how Edna had liked the boys. She said, "She loved Arlo." Arlo is their dog.

Good reports and bad reports

February 13, 1981

Our eleven-year-old twin grandsons had some problems on the school bus last week (the "boys will be boys" kind of trouble). A neighbor called Kiffaney and said that her girls dreaded riding the bus because of the twins. Kiffaney apologized for their behavior, then told the boys that they would have to walk home from school the next day because they had abused the privilege of riding the bus. Upon arriving home after their more than three-mile walk the next day, they came in full of enthusiasm saying, "That's fun, Mom— can we walk every day?"

Later in the week Kiffaney's heart missed several beats when the principal of the school called and asked if she and her husband could be in courtroom number 15 at the state capitol building the next afternoon at one o'clock. Kiffaney thought that the twins had done something really rotten and were going on trial or that she and Roger were being sued for damages or something. She asked the principal, "Could you please tell me the nature of the meeting?"

He replied, "We had a composition contest at our school, and Nathan and Tyler each won in their respective classrooms. And Tyler won the overall school composition contest."

The attorney general made the presentations, and it was very exciting for the boys' mother, who had expected the worst.

This reminded me of something my mother said about my brothers: "When Robert and Donald were little fellows, I used to wonder which one would grow up to be president, but the older they got, the more I thought we should be thankful if we could just keep them both out of jail!"

Obedience training for the school year
October 10, 1980

It seems that whichever kid has been with Grandma and Grandpa for summer vacation has been a little more reluctant to accept commands during the next school year. Could there be any correlation between the visits and the desire to do as they please?

Nathan brought a note home from school last week that his parents were to read and initial. It stated that Nathan had not cooperated with the substitute teacher that day.

Kiffaney said it was all she could do to keep from sending a note back to school for personnel to read and initial, saying that Nathan had not cooperated at home the same evening. She didn't do it— and more's the pity!

Mothers get such a kick out of everything their children say about their own children

May 28, 1981

Mothers get such a kick out of everything their children say about *their* children that calling them might almost be called "Dial-a-Laugh." Every time I talk to Kiffaney, there seems to have been some "crisis" with her children— or she's expecting one soon. But she generally seems able to roll with the punches and usually has put things into their correct perspective by the time she tells me about them!

Last week the twins brought home notes from school stating that their classes would be taking a field trip to Charleston at a cost of twenty dollars for each child. Because the family had toured Charleston at least five times, Kiffaney didn't think it was essential that the twins go. She told them that if they wanted to go badly enough to spend their own money, she would have no objections, but they didn't care to go that much, so the notes went back to school stating that the twins wouldn't be going on the field trip.

The next night, when Kiffaney was having a bridge party at their home, the phone rang, and the caller announced herself as the principal of the Dutch Fork School.

Kiffaney exclaimed, "Oh, dear, oh dear, oh dear!"

The principal assured her, "There's nothing wrong, Mrs. Frank."

Kiffaney replied, "Please wait a minute until my heart starts beating again."

The principal went on to say that the boys had said they couldn't go to Charleston because of the money, and she said that the school had funds to provide for the children whose parents couldn't. Kiffaney explained that she didn't think they would fit into that category. She said the twins had the money if they wanted to go but that they had been to Charleston many times with the family.

And bless Bradley's heart. He's our seventh-grade grandchild, who won first prize in the speech contest. After he won all three contests in his shirtsleeves, his parents stopped on the way home from the zone contest and bought Bradley a sport coat because the winner and his parents were invited to breakfast the next morning as guests of the Optimist Club, sponsors of the contest.

The contestants had to write original speeches, and it's not much wonder that Bradley's was a winner. The title was to be "Sharing," and does he know about sharing! Bradley wasn't quite two years old when his twin brothers appeared on the scene. That new sport coat they bought Bradley was in a "regular" rather than a "slender," which would have fit him better, because one of the twins is expected to fit into it within a couple of years.

Beauregard (a dog)

May 28, 1981

For about eight years our granddaughters have been begging, pleading, nagging and trying to shame Courtney and Suzie into letting them have a dog. The girls have had hamsters for several years, which their parents thought were respectable substitutes. But Lady Luck was with the girls two months ago when someone told them about a Golden Retriever that was looking for a good home. The weekend they heard about Beau, Suzie was at a Christian Women's Retreat at Colorado Springs, but Courtney and the girls went to visit Beau. The three of them fell in love with the dog but didn't have the courage to take him home until they had Mommie's consent. When she saw him the next day, Suzie melted, and he's part of the family now. Beau was a thoroughbred with papers, one year old, housebroken and had even been to obedience school. His mistress was moving into an apartment that didn't allow pets, and she had decided to give him away to anyone who could convince her that the new home would be a loving one.

I had thought previously that the only dogs people gave away were those that had never caught on to the house training bit. I thought the reason I loved our dogs was because it was such a relief when they finally realized it was more acceptable to relieve themselves outside than on our carpet.

Two coaches in the same family
October 15, 1983

One thing that Kiffaney and Roger do not enjoy is being coaches of the twins' soccer team. Nate and Ty (both thirteen) are great soccer players, so when the family moved to Cupertino, California, Kiffaney took them to an organizational meeting. Same old story: Everyone wants their kids to play, but they expect anyone other than themselves to be the coaches. For the twins to get to play, Kiffaney and Roger had to be the coaches. Kiff knew very little about soccer when she started, and Roger (who is a certified soccer referee) isn't crazy about other people's kids. Kiff and Roger each take one practice a week, and Roger coaches the games on Saturdays. The team has lost only one game so far (of eleven) in spite of the reluctant coaches.

Roger's birthday is this week, and Kiffaney is giving him a little refrigerator for his office, stocked with Pepsi. The only request that Roger made for his birthday was for Kiffaney to take both soccer practices this week.

On blowing your own horn
October 5, 1983

Our oldest grandson, Bradley, wrote us that this was going to be one of his best-ever years. He not only has his own bedroom and bath (which he shares with Arlo the dog), but his parents have rented a French horn for him. The school is furnishing him a French horn that he will keep at school, and he has the rented horn on which to practice at home. He thinks it's the height of convenience to be in the band without having to lug his instrument the mile he walks to and from school.

Do this kid's parents realize how lucky they are to have a fifteen-year-old who gets his kicks from blowing a horn?

The good news and the bad news
October 13, 1983

When I was talking to Kiffaney this morning, she told me both good and bad news about their thirteen-year-old twins. The good news is that Tyler and Nathan get to go on a week's science outing to Yosemite in February. They will do cross-country skiing and study different science projects. The trip is for eighth graders who carry A's in science.

The bad news is that the boys still enjoy using one another as punching bags. They were in the supermarket with their mother yesterday, pounding on each other at the checkout counter. The grocery checker said, "Boys, you are not permitted to fight in this store. Wait until you get home to hit each other."

Kiffaney said, "I prefer that they fight in here, thank you."

On a scale of . . .
October 12, 1983

After Bradley returned from a party the other night, Kiffaney inquired as to whether he had enjoyed himself.

Bradley said, "It was about an 8."

Kiffaney exclaimed, "That's good— 8 out of 10— you must have had a pretty good time!"

Bradley said, "No, Mom. It was 8 out of 100."

Our favorite artists

December 10, 1983

Tomorrow I'm to pick up some "grandchildren-painted" pictures from Jody's Framing Shop in Bellvue. We already have on display in our house over thirty framed pictures by our grandchildren. Maybe it's because I'm an old kindergarten teacher, but I prefer kids' artwork to adults' in most cases. We have five kid-painted pictures in our bedroom, two in the guest bedroom, four in the kitchen, and a regular gallery in the hall. Betty Vinton made me a sign that says, "Granny's Brag Wall," and it hangs in the center of our huge collection of grandchildren's artwork.

It's too late for those of you who put the grandchildren's art on the refrigerator door until it's faded, curled, torn, and ready to be thrown out— but children's art is delightful! A favorite hangs upstairs in our very old-fashioned bathroom. One of the grandsons did a picture of Granny in the claw-footed bathtub with one of her feet hanging over the side of the tub. He even included a big old light bulb hanging from an electric cord in the middle of the room.

They've done a picture of me getting my ears pierced and another during cherry pie baking season— depicting me looking very frazzled. The kitchen butcher block was copied exactly, along with bowls of cherries, stacks of crusts, and the rolling pin. Kids can be put to better use than just to plop in front of the TV or be sent to the swimming pool!

The amateur orthodontist

August 18, 1984

Several evenings while Tyler was here, he painted pictures for me. He did one great picture of hot air balloons (a whole group of them had gone over their home in Littleton, Colorado, while we were visiting there). Then he did a painting of Rick's truck, his fire pit, the camp at the farm, his workshop, and the rope swing.

Tyler had to be home Wednesday afternoon for basketball

Granny's cherry pies

practice and an orthodontist's appointment. His brother Bradley had got the braces off his teeth, and Kiffaney had always maintained that she would never pay for two in orthodontia at the same time. Now it was Tyler's turn. His mother said she had been watching the orthodontist very carefully and saving all of the wires that were used on Bradley so she could do Tyler's herself. Most kids would feel sure that their mothers were jesting with remarks like that, but with Kiffaney, her boys can't be sure. Kiffaney had given Tyler the choice of having his teeth straightened or getting new furniture for his bedroom. She's all heart! But he's feeling happy to have his own trained orthodontist at least.

Who's a soft touch?

May 24, 1983

Our son-in-law Roger has been in California for about ten days doing quite a bit of house hunting. He reports that the only houses he's seen where landlords will allow dogs are terrible. Kiffaney is leaving on Friday to help with the house hunt. She can't understand why five nice people should live in a dump just so they can have a dog in the back yard. It would be traumatic for the boys to give up their dog, and the only place they'd feel happy about leaving Arlo is with us. After they've been there a year and are sure they want to buy a home there, they will want Arlo back. They offered to pay us to have a fence installed in our back yard to keep their dog. (probably about the same week that Rick was planning to have a fence installed in our front yard to keep dogs *out*). Rick is a nicer person than I am, so, of course, he told Kiffaney we'd keep Arlo for them.

Actually, I'd keep an orangutan for Kiffaney and her brood.

Kiffaney has been taking care of all of the last-minute things that one has to do in preparation for moving clear across the country. She said that the boys have been pretty good, but the twins do poke at and wrestle with each other a lot. She had a little talk with them the other night and asked them if they had any suggestions as to how they might get along together better. They suggested levying fines for fighting or living in separate houses or living in separate states.

Bradley continues to be a great teenager. The awards night was held at his middle school last night, but he chose not to go because he had band practice with the high school band. This afternoon he went home from school with the six awards that he would have received from the stage last night had he gone. They were for citizenship, unselfish service, general scholarship, exemplary behavior, achievement for having a 96% or higher average in science and math, and achievement for having a 93% or higher average in English. He also came in second in the ninth grade class in a vote for "Student of the Year."

Tyler won the citizenship award for his homeroom.

Nathan's claim to fame is that he can spit farther out the bus windows than anybody else. That may come in handy sometime!

The Natural Beauty

A sixty-year-old natural beauty

April 7, 1977

Last week I had my big sixtieth birthday. Of all of the birthday cards and telephone calls I received, the only person who felt comfortable about saying the word "sixty" was my fifty-seven-year-old baby sister!

The market must be glutted with cards about people who aren't natural beauties, because I surely got lots of those. The theme tended to be "Here's to another year of . . . cold cream, mud packs, chinstraps, and low cal foods!" I was tickled by six or seven cards that depicted aging glamour girls on the front— and inside, scarecrows standing beside a wig stand. On the dresser were strewn false eyelashes, teeth in a glass, and bras padded up to about a size forty.

One place where the cards had me wrong is when they depicted a crew cut under the wigs. I think of my own glorious hair as being nearly to my waist, after letting it grow for several years, and I pile it on top of my head when I put on a wig. Bless Rick's sweet heart— he tells me all the time that my own hair is beautiful and I should face the world with it. I believed him once and ran down without a wig to Mulholland's for some groceries. Irene Pontow waited on me and we visited awhile. As I was picking up my purchases to leave, she said impersonally, "That will be $6.75."

I reminded her, "We run an account and pay once a month."

"What's your name?" she asked.

That did it. If my credit is no good in downtown Malvern without a wig, forget it!

And while in the Ozarks last fall at a bridge retreat, when I took off my wig the first night, my dear friend Clarky White, from Denver, was shocked to see my hair so long.

She questioned me, "Whatever are you letting it grow for?"

I replied, "I'm going to save it and sell it."

Then she countered, "Yes, but who's going to buy it?"

My friends realize that I need all the help I can get in putting my act together. Teresa Buffington called me as soon as she returned from a recent trip to California, excited about some Inga Borg false eyelashes that she had seen in a beauty parlor in Los Angeles. She brought me two pages of material and the addresses for ordering. The woman takes samples of a person's hair and makes the lashes of real hair to match your own hair exactly. Teresa said that they look simply beautiful. I guess I took the wind out of her sails when I exclaimed, "Oh, just what I always wanted—white eyelashes!"

Some fat ladies disapprove of weight losers

May 25, 1977

My mother told me that she had never lost five pounds in her life without some big fat woman telling her how much prettier she was before she had lost the weight. Something similar happened to me recently. I was in a group of some friends whom I hadn't seen for over a year. I had lost fourteen pounds, and two of my friends had gained a tremendous amount of weight. I carefully avoided staring at their figures while giving myself a mental pat on the back.

Then one of them came up close to me and asked, "Do those cracks in your face hurt?"

I responded, "I choose to call them character lines."

The other large lady declared, "Nobody has that much character."

Later I made a face, and the heavier one said, "When you

do that, you look like one of those wrinkled apple dolls."

I remained polite enough not to mention her bod, but I did say, "If you want me to say that I'm covetous of your plump face, forget it."

Having friends like that makes it neat for me to have a builder-upper like Rick for a husband!

One of my very overweight friends in Denver tells me that people constantly say to her, "Anna Mae, you're so well preserved— You don't have a line in your face!" She always replies, "If I see one little wrinkle starting to come, I hurry up and eat something!"

Thick hair or thin?

June 8, 1978

When we called Kiffaney on her birthday, she said that Judy (one of her old school friends) had flown in to spend her birthday with her. Both of Kiffaney's twins asked Judy questions that Kiffaney had rather they hadn't asked.

Tyler (the one who had to give up his bed to Judy) asked her, "Judy, just when are you going home?"

Then Nate (the other nine-year-old twin) asked her why she had hair above her lip. Judy had a good answer for that: "I have a thick head of hair on my head, and sometimes people with thick hair have it other places, too."

That should take care of all of the thin-haired women in our family. We don't have to feel conceited about not having mustaches!

Hot pink corduroy

January 10, 1980

Apparently I'm never going to get over my love of bright— even gaudy-colored— clothes. As far back as I can remember, it's been the brighter the better for me.

Everyone does not share these color preferences with me.

Last fall, after lunching at the French Cafe in the Old Market, Barb Taenzler, Ione Cook, and I stepped into the Clothes Out shop across the street from the restaurant. I spied a hot pink corduroy suit on a rack up front. Ione noticed it at the same time and remarked, "What an atrocious color!" Did I let that deter me? Absolutely not! I went out of there the proud owner of the only hot pink corduroy suit I had ever seen.

If I had originally planned on wearing it only for sporting events, that all changed. I even found myself wearing it to give speeches at ladies' luncheons the month before Christmas. And if I hadn't worn that, I would have worn a Kelly green crushed velvet suit or a bright turquoise one. Surely if that pink suit makes me look like an aging actress, I couldn't feel so great in it, could I?

I've thought a lot about three friends of mine who are hung up on your basic beige. How do they know when they have a new outfit? These ladies all have tiny figures, nice hair, and lots of good quality clothes. They are all happiest when they're wearing camel-colored clothing, but they do branch out into brown, with tiny accent touches of rust, and some gray. Are these basic beige ladies wonders of understated style and class, or are they merely color-blind?

It's not a yes or no answer

March 6, 1980

When Kiffaney and her oldest son were out walking last Sunday, Bradley told her, "I was about five or six years old before I ever saw Grandma Smith without her wig. I always thought her wigs were her hair until one morning I went into the kitchen very early, and a lady with long strands of thin hair was standing there. I looked at it and then asked Grandma what it was."

She said it was her hair, which she usually covered with a wig.

"Then," he said, "I told her that whatever she had been wearing was much better than her own hair."

He said that at the time he was too young to realize that

Granny's feelings might be hurt.

They walked on awhile, and Bradley asked, "Mom, do you like Grandma's hair better than her wigs?"

Kiffaney replied, "When I think of Mom, I always picture her in her wigs."

Bradley persisted, "That's not a 'yes or no' answer."

Kiffaney ended the discussion by saying, "Bradley, my hair is so similar to hers that I'd like to drop the subject."

Witch's clothes

June 25, 1980

The other evening Lenore, Terry, and Karl Hertz and Rick and I went to the most fabulous restaurant in the world, the A-Ri-Rung, up in the hills above Dodge Park. While we were riding along, Lenore asked me if I had gone golfing that day.

I told her, "Rick did but I didn't, because I was sorting out my clothes closet, trying to make room so my houseguests next week won't have to keep their clothes in their suitcases but will have room to hang them up."

"Don't throw anything out until I have a chance to go through them," Terry said, "We're always looking for Halloween costumes."

So I dress like I'm going to a Halloween party, eh, Terry? Watch your mouth!

Vera's home tailoring service!

July 6, 1980

If you're not perfect, you can get such a thrill out of doing a simple task correctly. Today I hemmed Rick's new trousers, and both legs miraculously turned out the same length. That may not sound like an accomplishment to some of you, but for me it was a milestone.

A couple of years ago, when Rick and I were in Scotland and England, I had taken a gold-colored knit Pendleton suit with me. The pant legs stretched outlandishly. I had a choice of rolling them up over my ankles or shortening them, and I decided in favor of the latter. I cut nearly two inches off the length of the slacks. Now, once a year, when we review that trip via our slides, I see myself as a tourist with one pant leg high atop my shoe and the other one touching the ground. It actually looks like my legs are two different lengths. Since that time we've taken our important alterations to Bonnie Pierce.

Today I slipped upstairs with Rick's new pants and measured and pinned and pinned (and carefully cut and cut). I didn't tell Rick what I was doing until I had finished because, had he known what I was doing, he might have been nervous and paced the floor outside the door.

They want my body
December 8, 1981

Many years ago I made the decision to donate my body (upon my death) to the medical school in Omaha, for the advancement of science. My friends, who try to keep me humble in any way possible, always have dissolved in gales of mirth and laughter at the mention of this plan. One of them always asks, "What would they want with that old bod?"

Now hear this: The last time we went to Denver, we stopped in to see my old school friend from Washington, Iowa, days—Wilma Febinger. Her son Dennis, who is a medical student, was visiting them at the time. I told him that I intend to donate my body to science and that my girl friends try to make me think that nobody would want this mis-shapen object.

Dennis asked me what surgeries had been performed on my body to date. When I told him "absolutely none," he informed me that they love getting bodies that haven't lost the gall bladder, appendix, uterus, or some other part. He said that by all means they'd want my body. And Dennis should know, too, because he already has his Ph.D. in biology, in which he specialized in the eye of the fish!

Where's the glue?

June 3, 1982

When I was a child in Washington, Iowa, my mother's aunts came twice yearly to sew for my sister and me. They were jolly fun ladies, but neither of them had half enough hair to cover the tops of their heads. In those days my sister Virginia and I hadn't realized that, although we had been blessed in many ways, we had been behind the door when the good hair was being passed around.

For the past sixteen years I've been able to face the world only because of the revival of wigs. A wayward wind has separated me from my crowning glory just three times: (1) on the first tee at the Air Force Academy golf course; (2) riding my bicycle between my home at the Van Pelt ranch and the Charles Plummer home, when a cattle truck went by and my wig whooshed right off my head and was lost in the ditch for some fifteen minutes; (3) last summer, when Rick and I were playing golf on the Avoca golf course with two polite couples who looked the other way until my hair was returned to the proper perch.

Last week my sister Virginia was walking between two office buildings near her work, loaded down with books and papers. Perched on her dome was a new Eva Gabor wig. On that day the winds in Denver were blowing at rates of more than 100 miles an hour. Those winds were no respecters of persons. Swoosh, swoop— and Virginia's beautiful hair left her head abruptly. She's lost wigs before, but not like this. That wind was tossing her wig like a balloon up, up and away! Virginia dropped her papers and books in hot pursuit of her hair. Her wig fell to the ground twice, and she touched it with a foot each time, only to have it take off again. Besides warehouse workers and office workers viewing her plight from the windows, there was a train in the yard, and the engineer gave her some glorious salutes with his whistle as the railroaders watched the determined career woman fighting to retain the well-groomed look with which she had left her office such a short time before.

All's well that ends well. Virginia did manage to capture her hair, put it in the proper place, and return to her office with quiet dignity.

Still another birthday!

March 31, 1983

When I was at bridge club at Jo Campbell's on Friday, I slipped away, while the others had lunch, and renewed my driver's license. The picture on my new license is flattering, and I was the only one at the license bureau at the time who had no restrictions put on the license. I don't even need glasses to drive. I was feeling good about the whole thing until one of the bridge club girls asked for how long the license would be good. I answered, "Four years, until I'm seventy." That sent the bridge club into hysterics.

Among my many nice and sentimental birthday cards were interspersed some silly thought-provokers. For example:

- From Doro Scott in Tucson comes the philosophy: "The secret to birthday happiness is learning to accept the aging process as something as beautiful and natural as premenstrual tension."
- Peg Gerould of Denver sent a card stating: "Happy birthday! Remember when we were *little* girls and wondered what we would do when we became *big* girls? Now we know." Inside, it said: "DIET."
- Barb Taenzler's card said: "Happy birthday! Thought about getting you one of those fancy ten-speed bikes, but at our age . . . who wants to be reminded of lighter frames and skinnier seats?"

Marilyn Burdic had a bridge luncheon honoring my birthday the week before, because she was going to be out of town at that momentous time. Maxine Waterman came from Mitchellville the Saturday before my birthday. We had a dinner party and bridge game that lasted until after two o'clock in the morning. Jo Campbell gave me such an interesting book, *"For Richer for Poorer,"* by Edward Stewart, that I started early one evening and didn't go to bed until I finished it at four o'clock that morning. Jo spoke for being the first to borrow this book after I finished it. Some gift givers are really cheap!

I share my birthday week with our three grandsons. The

twins (who will be thirteen) are inviting six friends each to their parties. They are going to play soccer, basketball, and touch football, and give prizes to the winning teams in each category.

I said, "It sounds like choosing up sides in gym class. I suppose if some boy isn't athletically inclined, he won't be invited."

Tyler agreed, "You've got it, Grandma. That's the way it is."

My oldest grandson, Bradley, who will be fifteen, doesn't want a party. In South Carolina children can drive alone in the daytime at age fifteen. What Bradley wants for his birthday is his driver's license, the additional car insurance that it takes to insure a teenaged boy's using the car, and the gift of driving the car all day long by himself.

The twins had ordered a white cake with chocolate icing, an angel food cake with chocolate icing, and a pineapple upside-down cake. Bradley thought he might order pork chops and rice for his birthday dinner, but one time his mother had cooked the pork chops a little too long and they were sort of dry, so he could hardly decide whether to take a chance on them.

Whoever said being a mother was easy? We grannies have more fun!

The face lift
February 21, 1985

It's becoming more and more common for ladies in the Midwest to have face lifts, nose construction jobs, and other cosmetic surgery. I would never want to do it because I'd hate to have a young face stuck with this comfortable old bod. But I've thought of one excellent alternative to having a face lift: just not looking at your reflection in the mirror any more than is absolutely necessary. Because I feel twenty years old—with the exceptions of the times I see the truth in the mirror—I thought up a super idea for the main floor bathroom at the farmhouse. Instead of a mirror or medicine chest over the pedestal sink, I had a window installed. Thus, I can wash my hands numerous times a day without confronting my countenance. Instead I look out west over the beautiful Iowa countryside. Around the corner is a mirrored and lighted medicine cabinet for Rick's convenience to shave. If I want, I can look, but I don't have to.

One of my shopping buddies is so much younger than I am that, when we go shopping together, the clerks in the stores ask her questions like, "Which one does your mother prefer?"

They ask me questions like, "Does your daughter live near you?" and "Does your daughter have children?"

This is the friend who just had her face and neck slashed in seventeen places while having her face lifted.

I said to her, "I suppose it wasn't enough for the clerks to mistake me for your mother. You won't be satisfied until the clerks start asking you what your grandmother prefers!"

Bridge Players Are
My Kind of People

Our bridge retreats

September 30, 1976

In 1959 three lady friends of mine and I and our children held the first of seventeen once-a-year bridge retreats at Green Mountain Falls, Colorado. A bridge retreat is similar to a religious retreat in that the people are dedicated to what they are doing and thinking, and they get to sit up as long as they care to without having to stop. We took a carload of food and clothes, and our husbands joined us on the weekend.

From this simple beginning, and as the children grew older, the bridge group eventually expanded to include twelve ladies and no children. We moved to the Moore Dale Lodge at Bailey, Colorado, did away with our cottage cooking, shortened the time to three days, and began eating the prepared meals in the lodge. Although we were surrounded by beautiful mountains, trees, and streams (not to mention the heated pool), we were scarcely allowed to marvel at our surroundings. If one happened to glance out the window and remark, "Isn't that a beautiful sunset?" or words to that effect, somebody would be sure to shout, "Shut up and deal!"

These retreats turned into endurance contests, too, as we always carefully counted the number of hours spent sleeping during the entire weekend and they usually added up to no more than five total hours. By Sunday night, when our bodies were returned to our families, we were walking zombies.

Things haven't changed too much over the years. The types of things we pack in our suitcases have changed from wave set, bobby pins, Midol, eyelash curlers, and chewing gum to Dentu Creme, Preparation H, Maalox, Rolaids, gout pills, diuretics, and potassium pills. The conversation has changed from little league ball and dancing classes to gall bladder and hysterectomy surgery.

Most of these friends have traveled extensively by now and have vacation homes. All of us have had our diamonds reset. The quality of our clothes has improved to compensate for the way our bodies have deteriorated. Wigs, false teeth, and glasses are rampant, and our memories are getting bad. I was appointed a committee of one to make name tags for the girls for next year. Also, they recommended that I bring my ear trumpet to next year's meeting.

The height of luxury

August 30, 1978

Saturday Virginia Stinard was entertaining at bridge and invited us to come an hour early to swim. I knew they'd added a room with an indoor pool just off the master bedroom, and I'd tried to picture it in my mind. My dreams weren't half as nice as the reality.

Besides the lovely pool, the windows are plentiful, and the ceiling so high that it reminded me of a garden room. As I was floating on my back, I counted sixty-four growing plants on shelves encircling the room.

It was neat at the beginning of a holiday weekend to not have to worry about a hairdo wrecked from swimming. I merely lifted mine off and left it on the dresser. This granny does indeed have more fun!

Group therapy for homemakers

September 28, 1978

Ten days of September found seven lady friends and myself enjoying ourselves at the Edgar Cooks' spacious Lake of the Ozarks home. From Glenwood we had Ione Cook, Mary Fernald, Jo Campbell, and Carol Dean. Marilyn Burdic and I were the Malvernians. Jacquie Schroeder, from West Point, Mississippi, and Clarky White, from Denver, completed the party.

The idea was for people to do what they feel is relaxing for them. The sleeping arrangements were made according to how long a person would want to sleep in the morning. Nobody was to awaken anybody at any time. Those who think that a vacation means sleeping late took the lower floor, and we idiots who awaken between five and six o'clock stayed upstairs.

The lake was smooth, and we spent over half of each day on the dock, in the water, or boating. I even learned to drive the Cooks' boat, which was a thrill. Ione, Mary, and Carol are water-skiers. There were excellent places for hiking, and several of us did some of that each day. One day we all went to see the "thong" trees—oak trees that were bent by the Indians when the trees were young, and tied with leather straps so the branches would point in the direction of the trail to the water.

Now that Jacquie is living hundreds of miles away, she thought it was safe to tell (amid hysterical giggles) what she and Marilyn Burdic used to do to me when Jacquie lived in Malvern. For some reason (I've never had a car wreck in my life) Marilyn and Jacquie preferred their driving to mine. When the three of us would go to bridge club in Glenwood, one of them would call and say it was her turn to drive. As we would be about to return home, the other one would say it was her turn to drive next time. Any time I would say it was my turn next, they would chorus: "You drove last time!"

The day we were going to the Garden Club walk in the forest (four miles from where we were staying), I decided to walk to the take-off spot, so I started out afoot ahead of the others. Enroute I noticed a car really hung up on a ridge, banged up and in a very precarious position.

When the others caught up with me, I inquired, "Did you see that poor car that was abandoned?"

They responded that Jacquie had noticed it and had said, "Look—I'll bet somebody picked up Vera and let her drive!"

One of my desires isn't the regular everyday wish of the majority of social security recipients. It's a pair of bib overalls. I had wanted some for two years, but every time Rick and I browsed in department stores, we would see them only in sizes five, seven, and nine. Lo and behold, I found a shop in Osage Beach that had bib overalls in my size, and even had a choice between blue denim and light beige carpenter cloth. I couldn't decide which I wanted most, so I bought both kinds.

When the cute young clerk wrapped them for me, she said, "These are all the bib overalls you'll ever need."

I was tempted to buy two more pairs then and there, to show her that there might be more life in the old girl than she thought.

Because our main theme on that vacation was "nobody has to do anything they don't want to do," I was reminded of another trip I took with my friend Clarky White, from Denver. Clarky called me, when I lived north of Glenwood, and said that United Air Lines was getting up a show plane to New York City to go to the latest Broadway plays. It was to last eight days and we'd see seven different plays.

I said, "I don't want to go on a tour thing and have people tell me where to go every minute and what time to go to bed and what time to get up. . . ."

Clarky replied, "It isn't that way. United arranges for the transportation, reserves rooms for all of us at the Americana Hotel, and gets all the theater tickets. You don't have to do anything you don't want to."

I agreed to go and flew into Denver to meet with the group. Clarky and I went to the airport several hours early, bought our accident insurance, ate two breakfasts, and went shopping.

When it was close to departure time, we went to the proper gate, which was surrounded by a mob. We must have been deep in conversation, because, when we glanced up, the big, beautiful show plane was taking off without us. We had thought that the people standing at the gate were the goers, and it turned out that they were only the wavers to the people going, who were already on the plane.

Clarky turned to me and, without cracking a smile, said, "See, I told you we didn't have to do anything we didn't want to. We didn't even have to get on the plane."

They were nice enough to put us on a TWA flight later in the day, and a United official greeted us at the New York airport, accompanied us to get a taxi, and gave each of us ten dollars for taxi fare into the city.

Do complete your ensembles
September 14, 1982

As I was going out our back door with my black bathing suit sprinkled with hot pink roses (all full-figured women seem to wear bathing suits with black backgrounds), I noticed that the rubber gloves I keep above the sink were also colored hot pink. I had just reached into the tea towel drawer for my hot pink bathing cap (doesn't everyone keep bathing caps in the tea towel drawer?), so just for kicks I grabbed the rubber gloves and wrapped them in my towel.

Imagine the stir I created when I made my entrance at the Stinards' inside pool in an outfit that included pink gloves! Virginia took a picture of my color-coordinated self. Now, does anyone know where I might buy hot pink flippers?

Some excerpts from another year at the Ozarks
October 6, 1983

The interests of the ladies in this group are as varied as our ages and dress sizes. Ages range from thirty-four to sixty-six, and dress sizes from four to forty-two. These ladies include avid water-skiers, tennis players, fisherwomen, golfers, joggers, those who exercise daily to exercise tapes— and we all love reading, singing, swimming, boating, eating, laughing, and playing bridge. Ann Demorey even drove her jeep into town daily to practice the piano at the Christian Church for nearly two hours. She was disappointed Sunday afternoon because the minister had gone somewhere with his family and had locked up the church.

Ann said, "I can't understand why you Protestants keep your churches locked."

I came back with, "It's to keep you Catholics from wearing out our pianos!"

I was the only senior citizen on the trip this year and took some razzing about my age. Fannie Foy told me several times that I was just two years younger than her mother. But I got my revenge on cute little forty-some-year-old Fannie. On the way home (five of us in Fannie's van), we stopped at Denny's in St. Joseph to eat. Just to elicit a chuckle, I ordered from the senior citizens' menu. When the waitress brought our dinners, though, she put the senior citizen's plate in front of Fannie. What a bang-up way to end a perfect six-day vacation!

Marathon bridge

March 30, 1985

This is March 30, and I'm anticipating a fun and wild day today. Fannie Foy and Ann Demory have invited twenty-four ladies to Fannie Foy's for another of the marathon bridge parties. We're to be there by one o'clock and stay for dinner and the evening— actually all night, if we wish. I'm riding to Glenwood with Marilyn Burdic, and I suggested last night (when the weatherman was predicting six to ten inches of snow) that we should perhaps take our nighties and bedroom slippers.

How wonderful to know so many good bridge players and fun-loving people. Mills County, Iowa, is definitely the garden spot of the world! Some of my friends who live other places have trouble getting together eight people for two tables of bridge.

Letters

Mamma cat

Dear Ashley, Bradley, Tyler, Nathan, and Kristin,

I know you'll all be sorry to hear that Mamma Cat died last Saturday afternoon. You all knew that she was very old (fourteen years) for a cat, and she had a very happy life and gave lots of laughs and pleasure with her antics.

She had practically quit eating and spent her last week in the basement, where she was nice and cool. She didn't appear to be in any pain but just wanted to sleep. Grandpa and I felt so badly about her and were trying to decide if we should have Dr. Ahern come and put her to rest permanently and painlessly.

Saturday we had been gone from home from one o'clock to nine, as we played twenty-seven holes of golf, then had a picnic with some friends. The first thing Grandpa did, when we got home, was to go to the basement to see Mamma Cat, and he called upstairs and said she was gone. She was lying on the child's buckboard wagon seat that is only about four inches off the floor, and she looked so peaceful.

Grandpa and I both cried— not for her but for us, who would miss her friendly homecoming greetings and her company in our evening porch-sitting, and her escorting us on our around-the-block walks in the evenings. She's the first cat I've known who would go for a walk with you, but she was highly selective. If you started to go off our block, she'd stop at the corner and wait for your return. Apparently, enough was enough for her.

You kiddies were born into a family that doesn't mourn the dead very much, because we all believe that there are hundreds of things worse than being dead— for instance, living in constant physical pain, mental illnesses, and incapacities; being slaves to drugs or alcohol; living in fear of anyone or anything; not being loved or appreciated; and on and on. To leave this earth to go to a better one isn't bad at all.

If people are kind and loving to their families while they're alive, then they can let them go in peace. Many times persons who seem unconsolable are selfish people. They aren't feeling sorry for the person who has died, but for themselves, who will be missing that person.

When someone can't be well, or active, or mentally competent, it's better for them to go. By the time you get to be my age, you'll be feeling that anyone who dies without going to a nursing home or hospital is a fortunate person— like my mother, who died at the bridge table while playing bridge with my brother, Bob, and two of her oldest and dearest friends. It was a shock initially to the rest of the family, but Mom would have loved going that way. I hope that I can go the same way, while I'm still having fun and planning things.

Anyway, Mamma Cat probably had pretty high cholesterol. About four years ago, when I switched to skimmed milk, Mamma Cat didn't like it. For one year I filled one section of her feeding dish with skimmed milk— and for one year she walked away from the milk, untouched. I finally decided to try her on half-and-half. She drank it and looked smug. From that day forward we bought a carton of half-and-half from our milkman twice a week.

We probably killed that cat with kindness!

Love,
GRANDMA SMITH

The dentist saga

May 3, 1977

Dear Son,

   While I was sitting in the dentist's chair today and he was picking away at the tartar on my teeth I started thinking about *your* teeth. It's been at least twelve years since I can recall hearing any mention of your seeing a dentist. Letting the tartar stay down in the gums can cause gum disease and deterioration. Do you want to lose your pearls?

   Since you did smoke for approximately eight years, I'm sure you have more tartar than most. I've never smoked, yet I have tartar when my teeth are cleaned every six months.

   If you'll go to the dentist and have your mouth taken care of, I'll gladly pay the dental bill rather than be disgraced by having a son with teeth in a glass before I have mine out!

Love,
BIG MAMMA

May 5, 1977

Dear Vera and Rick,

   I'm glad you wrote that letter to Courtney because I've been trying to get him to make an appointment with the dentist. He always has the excuse that he has no time: He's been so busy at the office; then we've been refurnishing the condo at Dillon; and by the time he golfs several times a week, there isn't much time left.

   Has Rick decided if he's coming out for the big member guest day in July at the Pinery Country Club? On Thursday everyone practices, then on Saturday and Sunday the scores count. Rick will have to send his handicap in advance for when Courtney signs them up.

   . . . The girls are fine.

Love,
SUZIE

May 9, 1977

Dear Suzie and Courtney,
    Would there be any reason that Courney couldn't go to the dentist on the Thursday they have the practice part of the golf tournament? Since Courney plays that course three or four times a week— and has for the past six or seven years— why couldn't he go to the dentist that day?

> Just courious,
> BIG MAMMA

May 13, 1977

Dear Mom,
    Get off my back. I was talking to Kiffaney last night, and she said that she's been trying to get *you* to go for a physical.
    Is it really true that you've never been back for your six-weeks' checkup after having Kiffaney?
    For shame!

> Your loving son,
> COURTNEY

Not too informative!

January 3, 1978

Dear Grandma and Grandpa,
    Thank you for the very nice letter. It was very thoughtful of you.
    To ansir your first question, the ansir is yes.
    To ansir your secon question the ansir is I don't know.
    To ansir your thrid question, it's yes.
    And the foreth is o.k.

> Love,
> NATHAN

(Unfortunately, I don't remember what I had written.)

Some messages on my sixty-eighth birthday

April 4, 1985

To Vera:

"Another year, another wrinkle." (Mary Click)

"Your birthday celebration is a good time to stop and consider this all-important question. . . . Am I wearing someone else's underwear?" (Barb Taenzler) (appropriate, since I'm bulging and bursting out of my clothes)

"Just think, no matter how old you get . . . I'll always be younger." (Peg Buffington Gerould)

"Don't think of it as getting older. Just think of it as another station on the Amtrak to Wrinkle City!" (Ardeth McLaughlin)

"Mother aside, you're one of my all-time favorite people. . . . I love you lots and thank you for teaching me how to play bridge . . . how to laugh, and how to appreciate life. . . . Having you for a Mom is like having a small slam every day! You're better than a good book!" (Kiffaney)

Who is this Vera Smith?

June 10, 1977

Dear Editor: (in response to my newspaper column and its accompanying artwork)

Your excellent paper has come to my attention way out here in Indiana. It really is well done, except for one small column. Who is this Vera Smith? She writes such exciting articles about going to sales, etc. I, too, enjoy going to auctions.

However, I can't see why you have on your staff such an absolutely ugly old hag sitting on an antique settee. I have a cousin by the name of Vera, and her maiden name was Stutsman. I lost track of her, but I would suggest that you bend every effort to find her and get her to write your articles. She could write equally well, and she is, or used to be, a beautiful woman. Her father was a medical doctor and treated me while he was still in medical school. Her mother was Nina, an absolutely gorgeous woman. With all these tips, I hope you can find my Vera and displace the old hag that you now have.

One more tip that may help you find her: On a recent trip to Iowa, since I attended Wellman High School from 1916 to 1918, I spent a day looking up old school notes published in the *Wellman Advance*. I found additional tidbits like the following:

March 29, 1917 (Kalona section)

Dr. and Mrs. E.E. Stutsman are rejoicing over the advent of a petite girl into their home. She came last Thursday, I believe. I've seen people just as happy because a boy came into their home as these folks are over their girl.

I hope that you don't resent my criticism. I just do this in the spirit of "keep America beautiful."

> Very sincerely yours,
> DR. GLEN R. MILLER
> Goshen, Indiana

My own letter to the editor

July 18, 1977

Dear Pete (Graham):

Since my cousin, Dr. Glen Miller of Goshen, got such fun out of popping up out of nowhere with his letter in search of his long-lost cousin, Vera, I'll claim him proudly. He taught for many years at the Mennonite college where many of our relatives were educated and taught. If Glen should happen by here sometime, he might see that I'm better looking than the hag picture that guides folks to this column. One reader (Letha Bayes) called and offered to write him a scathing letter in my defense. I think she thought he was serious.

He was so right about my mother being a beautiful woman. All the time my sister and I were growing up, we heard, "You'll never be as beautiful as your mother!" Sure enough, we weren't!

My parents' union was kind of a storybook romance. My

father, Dr. Eli Stutsman, was the young village doctor in Kalona, Iowa (a Mennonite settlement about the size of Malvern), and my mother was a high school senior.

They were married the July after Mom graduated from high school and took a six-week honeymoon in Colorado. They had a wonderful life together for fifty-three years and were blessed in many ways. They were especially blessed with good health, the ability to enjoy life to the fullest all of their lives, and they had absolutely hundreds of good friends.

I was born during a blizzard. My father delivered me, and (after two boys) his first words about me supposedly were, "Oh, it's a nice, fat girl!"

That's more or less the way it's been ever since, but I keep trying.

GRANNY VERA SMITH
Malvern, Iowa

P.S. to Glen: I loved the Wellman newspaper bit that you included in your letter about a petite girl having been born to Dr. and Mrs. Stutsman, because that's not the way I heard it!

Another cousin gets into the act

August 18, 1978

Dear Editor:

I enjoy reading your excellent newspaper but must take exception to the recent letter you received and published from Glen R. Miller of Goshen, Indiana. I, too, am a cousin of Vera Smith, nee Stutsman, and have seen her quite recently. She is still the beautiful, talented, witty, and charming girl of the 1920's and 30's whom my mother used to tell me about. (You see, she is much older than I.)

However, for a gal of her obvious age, she has held together pretty well. Therefore, Mr. Miller should relax, knowing that his Vera has been found, and try not to be disillusioned over the fact that she and the "old hag" are one and the same person. After all, beauty is in the eyes of the beholder.

Sincerely,
CHARLES G. IVES
Colonel, USA Retired
Placitas, New Mexico

Yet another response

September 2, 1978

Dear Pete,
We, too, enjoy the *Leader* from a far-distant place. We take exception to Dr. Glen R. Miller's (of Goshen, Indiana) criticism of our lovely Vera Smith.

1. Who does he know that in a rainstorm wears a wet suit and hunting boots over a Dior original to bridge club?
2. Who does he know that makes the slide down the Matterhorn at Disneyland seem dull compared to a ride in the car with her?

We would like to challenge him to a photographic contest decided by Leader readers' votes. We'll bet a Rebel flag that he's not one bit prettier than she!
As an AWOL member of the "Nobody's Perfect Club," I'm sure I speak for the whole group when I say Vera Smith helps keep America beautiful with her fun-loving spirit.
The question: Is Dr. Miller friend or enema?

Very sincerely,
The old school nurse,
JACQUIE SCHROEDER
West Point, Mississippi

Class reunion time

September 13, 1979

Dear Fellow Classmates,

Our class of 1939 is one of the four being honored during the homecoming reunion weekend.

I was thrilled, when reading a list of names of people in our class, to remember so many of you so well. At our age it's great to remember anything!

By having this four months' advance notice, we can exercise, diet, and place orders for various necessities. Some may need staunch foundation garments, chin straps, hearing aids, glasses, teeth, or hair.

Yank up your supp-hose and plan to see us at the reunion.

VERA STUTSMAN SMITH

On her birthday

October 30, 1979

Dear Kiffaney,

Words can never express what you mean to us on the eve of your thirty-third birthday, but I'll try. It's comforting to know that we can count on you for anything we'd ever want or need. It's your never missing an occasion to send cards, letters, and long-distance calls. It's feeling so welcome in your home and feeling free to discipline your children if we think they need it. It's your having married a wonderful man who's like another son to us. It's knowing that you have a feeling of self-worth enough so that you can be yourself at all times.

We're proud of you, Kiffaney. I feel sorry for everyone in the world who doesn't have a daughter like you. Happy birthday!

MOMMO AND RICK

I love him, so I told him so!

June 5, 1980

Dearest Rick,

There's no way I could find a printed birthday card that would begin to say how much I love and appreciate you. I appreciate you for being so ever dependable and willing to do everything and anything that you think would make me happy. I appreciate your young outlook on everything, your ability to tackle new hobbies, and your great skill at anything you undertake (like building the new deck and making our Scottish garden).

I love you because you're so sentimental and sweet toward all God's creatures. Who else cries for every bird that is cat-killed in our neighborhood? I love you because you're such wonderful company at all times. I've loved having you home all the time this first year of your retirement from work. I love you because the way you look at me makes me feel sweet sixteen!

I appreciate all of your smarts when we're working on crossword puzzles or word scrambles in the morning paper. I appreciate you for all the words you tell me the meaning of so I don't have to go to the dictionary. I appreciate you because you have such an appreciation for reading and readers. I'd be miserable married to someone who thinks that keeping little dust balls out from under the beds is more important than reading a good book.

I appreciate you because of your sincere belief in God and for the thoughtful prayers that precede each of our meals. I appreciate your overabundance of energy. I can't remember asking you to go anywhere or do anything and have you say that you were too tired. I appreciate you because you're such a fabulous host to all of our company.

I wouldn't change a thing about you on your sixty-fifth birthday. And to think that I used to believe love was mostly for the young!

All my love,
VERA

74

A letter to a mother-in-law

October 8, 1981

Dear Vera,

It's been few weeks since Kiffaney came back from her trip to Malvern, but she's still "up" from the experience. It really meant a lot to her to visit with you and Rick. I envy her in that special friendship you have. I've been thinking how good an influence you've been on Kiff all these years. She's now a product of the many years she spent with you, growing up, and the many years she and I have shared together. But the things that really make Kiffaney special to me were there from the first day.

Then I thought about how happy each of my sons is when it's his turn to visit you and Rick. There is nothing more special to them than that summer visit. Both of you have had such a good, positive influence on them. Their respect and love for you has reinforced those principles they see when they visit. Those same principles— among them, love, honesty, humor, and zest for living— are the same I try to instill.

Finally, I turn to myself. Knowing you and Rick all these years has done me a lot of good personally. You have trusted me, from the start, with your daughter's happiness— a responsibility that I've always taken seriously. You've always been helpful when we needed it— and even when we didn't. Even the treasured antiques that you gave us have helped to make our house a home, thanks to you.

I know Kiff may have said it before, but I feel I'd like to tell you myself how much I appreciate all the good things you are and have done for all of us. We love you a lot.

Love,
ROGER

Kiffaney's college roommate visits

August 5, 1982

Dear Smiths,

Just a little note to thank you for letting me come and visit you and Kiff. Your house and your small town are wonderful, and I enjoyed being there. Thanks for putting up with my bridge game. Maybe the next time we play, I will have mastered the game.

While Kiff has always told me wonderful things about her mom, she hadn't told me enough about Rick. He is one of the nicest persons I have ever met. Thank you again for letting me come and be a part of your family.

I thoroughly enjoyed all of the cut flowers in your house, even in my bedroom and the upstairs bathroom. I also enjoyed eating by candlelight from your Haviland dishes. It made me feel like a visitor in an English manor and appealed to my romantic ideas of times that were always elegant.

Have a great summer, and I'll think of you every time I go to a flea market.

Sincerely,
EDNA SLOAN

To my son on your birthday

April 7, 1983

Dear Courtney,

On April third you will be thirty-nine years old. On their children's birthdays mothers sometimes like to savor the entire lives of their children, and I'm a mother.

You were lucky. The longer I live and the more I learn of life, the more I realize just how lucky you were to be truly wanted by both parents. Clever of you to wait until we had been married thirty-six months to put in your appearance. We were so anxious for a baby by that time that we would have settled for just any ordinary baby. You didn't need to be as wonderful as you are! I was so thrilled to be pregnant that I hated to nap or go to sleep at night for fear that when I awakened, my pregnancy would turn out to be a dream.

We were prepared for you, too, with a brand new five-room house with two bedrooms and an attached garage. For all of that luxury, back in 1944 we paid only $3,250 (not $32,500, but actually $3,250). Our house payments were $36 every month. By the time I was two months' pregnant, we had purchased your first wheels— a maroon English peram- bulator. Was that some buggy! Can you imagine spending triple the cost of our monthly house payments for a baby buggy?

From the day you arrived, you were the moon, stars, and sun of our lives. You were born at Fitzsimons Army Hospital in Denver, where your dad was an army officer. You were less than two when World War II was over, and we returned to Iowa for three years. When you were five and Kiffaney was three, we came back to Denver and purchased the home where we lived for twenty-five years.

The neighborhood into which we moved was alive with kids, especially boys your age (Mike White, Chum Scott, Jack, Jim, and Joe Harlow, Johnny Anderson, Bob Swisher . . .). You had a wonderful, carefree two years of play with your neighborhood friends, and I (who was a kindergarten-pri- mary teacher) didn't send you to preschool or kindergarten. I just let you live, breathe, and play with your friends, until Kiffaney, at age four, was dying to start to school. Your first school experience was that same year in first grade at age six- and-one-half. I don't want to embarrass you, but your baby sister had to teach you how to tie your shoestrings before you started to school.

Life for you has always appeared to be a bowl of cherries. You always picked up friends and championships effort- lessly. Everything came easily for you, and you always accepted it as your due but never grew conceited. You've al- ways been kind, considerate, and aware of the feelings of others. You're a fabulously successful businessman and fearless in taking chances in investing. Although you work long hours, the happiness and comfort of your wife and chil- dren have always been of number one importance to you. You've been a dream of a son, an ideal brother, husband, and father. Who could ask for more?

Happy birthday, Courtney
from your big Mamma

P.S. I have one confession to make to you, Courtney. I

didn't attend any of your graduations (not from eighth grade, high school, or college). I know you thought I did because I was always there afterward all dressed up and beaming about the great graduation ceremonies. But the truth is that those things are so boring and your classes were always so large that I probably couldn't have picked you out of the crowd anyway, so I just drove around in my cool car, then appeared in the crowd after the speeches were over.

Dear Dr. Kammandel

August 31, 1983

Dear Dr. Kammandel,

On August 19th I was in your office with a bladder infection. You said that you'd send me the results of the urinalysis in a letter the next week. So far I haven't received any correspondence from your office except for a Medicare blank to be filled in. You prescribed Bactrim DS enough for one week, and it worked miracles in clearing up the infection.

The reason I'm writing this is because (since my doctor Mary Cpizzi has left Glenwood) you are now my bladder doctor. I'm going to the Lake of the Ozarks with eleven girl friends to play bridge, diet, walk, swim, boat, and laugh, from Sept. 9th to Sept. 17th. I often leave home without my American Express card, but I refuse to leave home without my bladder pills. How do I go about getting a prescription for same? My life is so neat and so worth living, and I don't want to die out of town with pain from a bladder infection! Help!

The theme of our bridge retreat, which has been going on for ten years, is that nobody has to do anything that they don't want to and nobody wants to leave one minute before the planned departure time. Thus, were I to die of a bladder infection, nobody would leave early just to bring my body back. They'd probably tie me by my leg to the dock until their vacation was over.

Sincerely,
VERA SMITH

Letters from relatives

September 2, 1983

When I opened our mailbox this morning, I noticed that Bradley's letter was addressed to just "Grandma and Grandpa" (no last name), but he did have our correct box number on it. Tyler's letter was addressed to "G. and Grandpa Smith," Kiffaney's was addressed to "Mom-o and Rick Smith," and our niece Jody Stutsman's was addressed to "Auntie Vera Smith." Do they all think their mail won't be delivered without stating what relation they are to us?

Tyler's was a thank-you letter for the vacation he spent with us last week. He told us about the dance he'd gone to the night before. The girl he likes wasn't there, so he danced with two other girls.

Bradley was telling me all about a cruise that their family went on Sunday that took them under the Golden Gate Bridge and the Oakland Bay Bridge, as well as alongside Alcatraz and San Francisco.

Our niece Jody's letter gave us the dates of her two-week vacation. She's coming out to spend it with us between the time she finishes her law school classes and when she graduates from law school.

Kiffaney said they were so happy for Nathan this week. He hadn't received honors the last three times that Tyler won them. Tuesday night the parents were invited to a recognition ceremony at school. The students get points for each extra-curricular activity in which they participate. Then, if they have enough points plus being on the Scholastic Honor Roll, they get a large letter. Nathan won awards for being the "most valuable member of the wrestling team," "most valuable member of the basketball team," and also twenty points for being captain of the basketball team.

Kiffaney went on, "Tyler has been wonderful since his visit with you. We really, really appreciate your welcoming him and showing him such a good time! Again, I feel so sad that you are so far away when we all could enjoy and appreciate you so much— but then you will be out here soon, and that will be nice."

And, in closing: "I thank you so much for giving me so much in spirit as well as worldly goods."

Lots of love,
KIFFANEY

An open letter to my mom

September 15, 1983

Tuesday I received a letter from Harold Schneider of Seattle. He had seen a column of mine in the *Washington Evening Journal* and inquired if I remembered him from our old neighborhood days. He went on to say that he never forgot how our mother read to all of the neighborhood kids, on our back porch steps, when it was hot in the summer.

It was wonderful for you to be remembered for something like that sixty years later, and it sounded so typical of the types of things you did. The last twenty years of your life you got letters from several of the girls who had been in your Girl Scout troop, of which you were the leader for twenty-three years. You also heard from various girls who'd been in your Sunday School classes and missionary groups. Many said that your parties, picnics, and camping trips were some of their fondest childhood memories.

I don't believe I realized until after I'd gone away to college that everyone's mother didn't play baseball or golf or go fishing, hiking, and picnicking at the drop of a hat.

Auction Sales

Auction sales are exciting hobbies

March 18, 1976

A fun and exciting hobby of Granny's and Grandpa's is going to local farm auctions. It's far more fun than my recollections of the circus, carnivals, or the chautauquas in my girlhood days. There's no admission charge, and the people are much friendlier and more interesting. It's nice seeing many of the same people over and over and getting to know what certain people will be trying to acquire.

When they go to a sale in threatening weather, people are always hopeful that there'll be a sleeper (a good article that goes ridiculously cheap.) The best luck I ever had in that way was the frigid, snowy day when I was able to get a wicker baby buggy (over 100 years old and very ornate) for the sum of seventeen dollars. The only similar ones I'd seen were priced in the two-hundred-dollar range. But, remember, the weather was below zero, and there were very few women standing out that day. Possibly this item wasn't a necessity for a grandmother, but it certainly is a conversation piece as a magazine holder in our living room.

Even if you aren't buying, sales are interesting, because you can put a hypothetical price on each object the auctioneer puts up for sale, just to see how far wrong you are about the price. But auctions are not quite as much fun for Rick as for me because he has the job of lifting the purchases into the truck and finding a spot to put the relics in our home. He says if I buy one more chicken incubator, I'll have to start hatching baby chicks.

A big Saturday night in Malvern

July 1, 1976

About once a month the Malcolms and the Jameses hold an auction at the local community building. These started very insignificantly, but they have gradually grown in amounts of things gathered together— until five hours wasn't enough to finish the sale on Saturday night.

When I bicycled downtown for the mail on Saturday morning, Teresa Buffington hailed me and suggested that we drop over to the community building and see what was being offered for sale that evening. She said she had seen an ad of theirs offering wicker furniture. We agreed to meet there that night about an hour before sale time, to get a good seat.

One of the odd things about an auction is that there are many things you really want that you hadn't thought previously about needing. For example, we bought a child's buckboard wagon seat for thirty dollars less than the one I had seen at the last antique show in Omaha, and it was only the second one I had ever seen. Another thriller was a bright red scooter the likes of which I hadn't seen for fifty years, and in excellent condition. Now I can scarcely wait for the two granddaughters to get out here and see if *they* aren't thrilled about it.

The baby buggy

The good wicker furniture was saved for midnight, and that held the crowd. I think lots of people could envision it painted and sitting in their family rooms, sun rooms, or glassed-in porches.

It always takes another twenty minutes or so after a sale for Rick to help some of the ladies (with husbands home baby-sitting) load their goodies into their trunks and pick-ups. Rick appears to be having fun at the sales, but sometimes I suspect that he half wants to go and mostly thinks some people are not safe to turn loose at such places! I did kind of glance his way, after I nodded my head "yes" for an old stove at the Hasselquist sale, and decided from the stricken look on his face that a warm husband would surely be preferable to a cold old stove. The stove went to the next bidder.

Then *we* had an auction

July 21, 1983

It's happening, folks! Monday, July 25th at five o'clock at 507 Lincoln Avenue in Malvern, we're having an auction sale. You could almost call it a "forced sale" because the neighbor's garage (where we've been keeping two of our cars) is up for sale and we don't have parking space at home for two more cars. I've long wanted to clear out our lovely oversized garage for cars, and now that Brian Weeks is our summer handyman, it's the perfect time to do it.

Our garage started filling up about ten years ago when Rick and our nephew, Freddie Emmerling, and I went to an antique auction in Iowa Falls in the pickup truck. We bought a beautiful buggy with oak spoke wheels. We intended to hitch up Prince to it and drive it around. Prince agreed to pull it, but we've never gotten the single harness and all that it takes, so one car was displaced in the garage to house the buggy. Gradually we had filled the basement, back porch, and garage with antiques and some junk, so the time had come to clear out.

Antiquers—who can't remember where they spent last

"2 dollar, 2 dollar, 2 and a quarter?"

Thanksgiving— never forget, to the dollar, what they paid for an antique. We even remember what vehicle we were driving the day of the purchase or whether someone else hauled the beauty home for us. The kitchen cupboard that is going in the auction was purchased at a sale in Red Oak about six or eight years ago, where I went with Teresa Buffington. Harvey Chaney hauled it home for me. The 1910 "Gee Whiz" washing machine that was made in Des Moines used to be my most prized possession. I thought it was adorable when I spied it at a gigantic auction in the Glenwood armory. I couldn't stay for the sale, so I had my neighbor Mary Click bid the machine in for me. John Dean and Bob Buffington loaded it into Mary's car for her laughing every step of the way because it was mine and not their wives'! I have used it ever since as a clothes hamper in the upstairs bathroom. It is quaint and cute, but all of a sudden it just looked dirty to me. I think it's because Brian Weeks painted that bathroom such a sparkling clean white.

The Shirley Temple pitcher, mug, and bowl bring memories, too. I saw them in an antique shop, and they were reasonably priced so I made a down payment and put them on "will-call." Antique dealers are usually very nice about keeping articles for picking up later, but when I returned for my treasures, the dealer couldn't find them anywhere. She pretended to search and search. She probably realized she had sold them too cheaply, but I don't like making a fuss, so I left. When my friend Maxine Waterman came for the weekend, I told her about it. She was furious and went to that shop. I don't know what she said, but she came back with my three pieces of Shirley Temple glassware for the price that the dealer had quoted in the first place.

The antique organ holds lots of memories, too, but I don't play it anymore. When we lived in La Porte City, Iowa (right after World War II), my husband and I bought the organ out of an old country schoolhouse. We hadn't refinished it but just enjoyed playing it and having it. When we moved to our condo, there wasn't room for both the organ and the baby grand piano, so we decided to keep the organ. The man who refinished the organ agreed to take the piano as payment for the refinishing job. He did a gorgeous job on that organ.

After the sale

July 28, 1984

The sale went unbelievably well. The total amount we took in was four times higher than what we had anticipated. Antique dealers bought practically everything. We found out that antiques are indeed a good investment. I heard the auctioneer cry "sold" on the antique organ at fourteen fifty. I thought that was $14.50, but it was $1,450.

Those Shirley Temple glass pieces floored me. I had paid seventeen dollars for the three pieces (thanks to my gutsy friend Maxine.) The morning of the sale, we had received a call from a man in Clarinda, inquiring about them. About two o'clock in the afternoon the man appeared, to inspect the glass pieces. He hovered around all day, then lost them to a dealer for $150. The wicker doll buggy (not to be mistaken for my gorgeous full-sized 100-year-old buggy) for which I had paid $10 went for $150. The kitchen cupboard I had bought for $24 went for $315.

It was something like being in dreamland sitting on my back porch and hearing these people fighting to pay us money for cleaning out our basement, back porch, and garage. I spent part of my time setting the tables for my sit-down dinner for twelve that I gave my helpers as soon as the sale was over.

Brian cleaned out the garage yesterday and Rick had two cars in there last night.

When Brian came to work this morning, I met him at the gate with two buckets and he helped me pick cherries. I had made about a dozen pies for the freezer, before all of this business about the sale came up. I just couldn't stand to see the rest of the cherries go to waste. After stuffing a pie down Brian and Rick, giving pies to Mary and John Click, Virginia and Don Primrose, Marilyn and Alan Burdic, Sarah and Don Aistrope, Peg and John Phelps, Irene and Chuck Cowell, Margaret Ann and Bob Hageman, Betsy and Bill Johns, Verna and Dan Swaboda, we still had another dozen pies to freeze.

The day of the sale, Lauraine Breeding had offered us the use of a kitchen table, as all of our own furniture was covered with items. You guessed it— the auctioneer sold it. We may give Lauraine what we receive from selling her table, but only if she agrees to pay us the auctioneer's fee!

Buying again

Summer of 1985

Tuesday I had a marvelous time at an auction sale in Emerson. I had spent all the day before telling myself that I didn't want to go, that it was too hot, and on and on. My final word at bedtime Monday night was that I didn't want anything, didn't need anything, and couldn't afford anything. But came the dawn— I jumped out of bed at six-thirty, called my neighbor Lauraine Breeding, whom I knew wanted to go, and told her we were taking off at eight o'clock. I'm so glad we did!

It's fun seeing all of my regular sale-going friends, as well as meeting and talking with people from Missouri, Kansas, and other states who occasionally turn up for extra good sales.

Until one o'clock I bid on only one thing, a child's antique sled, which I didn't get. But I was really in luck about two o'clock, when the old washing machines came up for sale. We're now the proud owners of an 1880 vintage rocker washing machine. It still has the original printing on it. It's almost entirely wood, and, by using a block of wood to keep it from rocking, we have an adorable bedside table for the lamp, next to the brass bed in the master bedroom at the farmhouse. I just know that Rick is thrilled about it, too, but he did manage to conceal his excitement quite well.

While I was at the sale, Rick put up hooks for a hammock between two big pine trees at the side yard at the farmhouse. That's the coolest place in the state of Iowa.

Holidays

Halloween

November 4, 1976

One of my favorite holidays, Halloween, has come and gone again, and I masqueraded for the children who came trick or treating. I always base the costume on my own stringy hair (the envy of any Halloween witch). Several times before, I've colored my hair green, with food coloring, but Rick didn't like that, so this year I dyed it turquoise blue. I can make myself look grotesque without a mask, so I usually go that route. I cut some buckteeth out of a raw potato and molded a cube of margarine over my own already prominent nose.

The margarine began to get soft and melt, and at one point it was covering my nostrils. Because my mouth was jammed with the potato teeth, my ability to breathe was touch and go for a while.

After two hours of the little trick or treaters, it was time to clean off my face and go gypsy-style to the Halloween party at the church, where I had been asked to tell fortunes. This was thrilling for me because these kids were so fresh and interesting and seemed to have so much potential that it was easy to foresee marvelous futures for them. I may have made some inroads into future population control, too, because I dealt them out families limited to one and two children in most instances. I did give one thirteen-year-old girl the prospect of having six children, but she'll be able to handle them. She's going to be a Miss America and then have a fabulous public-speaking career at clinics and schools, speaking to children on subjects of motivation and making the most of oneself.

Last year it took me three weeks to get all the green out of my hair, but few people knew it, as my wigs covered it. Believe me, Halloween is the only day of the year that I have found any use for my own hair!

Thanksgiving blessings

November 23, 1978

I am thankful that . . .

We believe in God, this country, our families, our friends, and ourselves.

We have the gifts of excellent health and the energy for everything we want to do.

Our lives have been increasingly more interesting and happy with each passing year.

We live in the most ideal spot in the whole world— a small midwestern town in a quaint old house surrounded by wonderful neighbors.

Our children are such a source of pleasure, and that they did such bang-up jobs of choosing their life mates.

We have five healthy, happy, intelligent grandchildren and the nervous systems and senses of humor to permit each of them to visit us several weeks a year without their parents.

The pleasure derived from my two favorite pastimes, reading and walking, continues to increase as the years go by.

I am also happy that my husband . . .

Always looks at me like I'm a super special lady.
Prefers *my* company for everything from golf to traveling.
Loves my relatives— even those who are not easy to love.
Worries unashamedly any time I'm on the highway alone.
Thanks me after each meal I prepare for him.

Praises the things I do that deserve praise, and lots of things that don't.

Loves me more than anyone else in the world and treats me as if I'm a national treasure.

Christmas without kids

December 26, 1978

We had a fabulous Christmas in spite of the fact that several people thought I would wither and die from being minus any of our children or grandchildren on Christmas Day. Each morning the entire week before, Rick would say, "Honey, are you sure you won't be unhappy being away from the kids at Christmas?"

I'd ask, "What kids?"

How could we possibly be lonely with the kinds of friends we have? Sunday we were invited to Carol and John Dean's in Glenwood, for their traditional turkey dinner and all the trimmings (including two grandmothers and lovely children) on Christmas Eve. Then we all went to the candlelight service at eleven o'clock at the Methodist church.

Christmas Day we had a delightful time having Christmas dinner with our neighbors, the Clicks. Mary's parents and her sister Nancy were also guests. We had some wild games of Hearts after dinner.

It was a very merry Christmas. Christmas isn't being any particular place. Rather, it's a feeling that people care about you and you care about them. You can have this feeling sitting alone in a stalled car or in a mob of wall-to-wall people at a shopping center.

The kids' Christmas

January 18, 1979

Kiffaney wrote that, because of additional train equipment that Bradley got for Christmas, it is no longer possible for him to share a room with anyone. A room off the family room housed the furnace and had many shelves full of Roger's spare electronic equipment. It was also Arlo the dog's room. It's heated and carpeted. They moved Roger's equipment to an outside shed, painted the walls, and— Presto— a fourth bedroom. Bradley and Nathan both wanted the room so they could sleep with Arlo. They cut cards for the privilege, and Nate won. Then he sold the use of the room to Bradley!

That Christmas gifts sometimes create problems reminded me of the Christmas when we bought Courtney a large pool table, before we built on the family room. I had never played pool and didn't know that a player had to stand at least a cue's length back from the table. So on Christmas morning Courtney's desk went out first, then his bookcases, then his chest of drawers, and finally his bed. Fortunately, he also got a sleeping bag for Christmas.

I was reminded that every man I've ever known enjoys talking about the many hardships he had as a boy. For example:

- They all walked at least seven miles to school, fall, winter, and spring.
- They stacked all the wood used for the entire winter.
- They never slept less than three to a bed until they were twenty-one years old.

I told Courtney that Christmas that although he might miss his bed, it would all be worth it later in life because he could now tell his children how rough he had it. He can say that, as a boy, he didn't sleep in a bed— he had to sleep in a sleeping bag under a pool table!

Thanksgiving thoughts from the grandkids

December 6, 1979

From Kristy (age eight):

> I am thankful for:
> Being alive.
> Having parents (nice).
> Having food.
> Having a nice sister.
> Being healthy and skinny.
> Having money.
> Having alive grandparents.
> Having a hamster and horses.

From Tyler (age nine):

> I am thankful for:
> Clothes Food Water
> "Candy" every bit
> Shelter good
> Family Schools Milk

From Bradley (age eleven):

I'm thankful to have Mom and Dad as my parents and Nathan and Tyler as my brothers. I'm thankful to have such wonderful and kind grandparents like you. I'm thankful to have aunts and uncles and friends. I'm also thankful to live in such a nice house and neighborhood. I'm thankful to be able to learn and to go to school. I'm thankful for being smart and having a good mind. I'm thankful to have a dog. I'm thankful to have nice clothing and furniture. I'm thankful to be able to raise some guppies—By golly—I have so many things I'm thankful for, I couldn't possibly list them all!

Granny is thankful, too, the week after Thanksgiving
November 30, 1979

For:
>Freedom and a loving God.
>Good health.
>Loving husband and family.
>Friends who are a riot and can laugh at themselves (and at me.)
>Being in a location where we can watch the wild geese flying south.
>Return of the yellow finches to our finch feeders.
>Most beautiful and plentiful crop of bittersweet ever seen.
>Being listed above the hamster on Kristy's list of "things to be thankful for."

Reflections of 1979
January 3, 1980

With so many people bad-mouthing the year just ended, I decided to reflect on pleasant things about old 1979.

1. Freedoms of opinions, worship, speech, and lifestyles were still ours in 1979.

2. Weather and rainfall for crops were very nearly ideal in Iowa in 1979. Although fuel supplies are lessening and becoming more expensive, we had the mildest fall and December that we've had in thirteen years. There were four days of good golf weather the week before Christmas, and that many after.

3. Twelve lovely, framed pictures painted by our grandchildren were added to our house decor. They were very tastefully framed at Jodi's in Bellvue, where some customers had actually attempted to buy some of them.

4. I'll always remember 1979 as the year that Rick very wisely decided to retire early so he could enjoy his numerous hobbies full time. It's been marvelous to be able to do exactly

as we please. Every day is a weekend. We can stay up until two o'clock and sleep in until ten o'clock. When we go on a trip, we're the ones who decide when we'll start home and how long we'll take getting home. I am thrilling to all of my refinished and mended pieces of furniture and bric-a-brac that Rick rejuvenates in his basement workshop.

It's a secure feeling to know that I won't have to miss any of my bridge clubs this winter because of bad roads. Rick will just put chains on the pickup, and off we'll go. I really appreciate Rick's hiking with me sometimes, too. I suspected it isn't his favorite pastime, because Thursday, when we walked out the Blue Grass Road, turning right at Ted Bowen's, then right again past Lola Hasselquist's, Rick muttered, "If I had liked walking, I could have stayed in the army."

We're so pleased with Mills County living. I don't understand people who retire, then move away from familiar friends, things, places, and smells. I even miss the odor of hogs when we vacation too long out of state.

5. One of the neatest things that happened in 1979 was our getting the big red Toronado convertible. We admire it too much to drive it. In fact, one of my readers from Washington, Iowa (Rachel Jungbluth) wrote: "Haven't heard anything about Big Red lately. Often thought that when you put him up on blocks, you could have him customized with shelving, drawers, bins, secret hiding places, etc.— a sort of Vera S. and Frederick G. Smith Memorial Library. Useful, too, in case Rick's den fills up again."

My 1980 Thanksgiving list

November 27, 1980

1. The hundreds of choices I'm afforded concerning my day-to-day living.

2. A husband who not only understands me but treasures me.

3. Children to whom we feel close enough to give advice, and who feel close enough to us to ignore that advice and do as they darned well please.

4. Grandchildren still young enough that they haven't outgrown loving to come to our house.

5. This neat old house that lends itself so well to antiques and also to the ever-present cobwebs and the dust balls under the beds that a habitual bridge player inevitably collects.

6. My many friends who have this world's greatest senses of humor, who are always predictably good company, who can laugh at themselves, who are not petty, and who do not have a jealous bone in their bodies.

7. Our location in small-town midwest America.

8. The capacity to enjoy and appreciate each wonderful day and the good fortune of being married to Rick, who has the corner on the most hobbies and interests of anyone I know, plus the physical stamina to enjoy them all.

Our grandsons, the junk dealers!
January 15, 1981

Kiffaney and Roger and their three sons, from Columbia, South Carolina, were with us for the Christmas holidays. The boys love coming to Malvern, and we can't anticipate beforehand what wonderful thing will impress them most on any one visit.

Monday Kiffaney, Roger, Rick, and I took off about noon for shopping, leaving the boys with instructions for their lunch and saying we'd be gone several hours. We didn't get home until nine o'clock.

Tuesday we all went to the Firehouse Dinner Theater to the excellent matinee of the musical *Oklahoma* and the buffet luncheon. It started snowing halfway through the performance, and we had a skiddy ride home from Omaha. That was the night of Barb and Jake Taenzler's Christmas party, but they realized we had houseguests.

Wednesday (Christmas Eve) we invited Sarah and Don Aistrope and Lottie Ruse to come over for a steak dinner with us. Sarah brought her homemade candy in about seven different varieties, and that's something I cannot resist.

Kiffaney and Roger bounded up from the dinner table,

cleared it, and did the dishes, while the rest of us were sitting visiting. Kiffaney told me later that Roger asked her, "Am I expected to get all the foreign matter off these pans, or just what was baked on today?" If I were a clinic-clean house-keeper, I wouldn't enjoy having grandchildren— even junk dealers— anytime they're available.

We had a glorious Christmas day with the traditional turkey dinner and all the trimmings. I'm sure that all of us received lots of presents that we didn't even know we wanted. Among the things under that category for me were the bumper stickers for all of our rolling stock; they say "Grannies Have More Fun."

Two days after Christmas Kiffaney and Roger flew to Denver and left the boys with us for five days while their parents recharged their batteries and regrouped to start coping in 1981.

Rick and I had checked with the boys' parents via phone before Christmas, to be sure that we bought the boys all the things they really wanted— like the ball-bearing shoe skates for outdoors, Legos® space station, and construction ma-chinery (those marvelous building sets that cost just a little less than building a county bridge). But it all paled beside the fabulous discovery that the boys made the weekend after Christmas, in the form of the Iowa bottle and can law. They had never heard of the idea of going anywhere and picking up empty bottles and cans, and being paid for them at the local grocery store. The unusually mild winter helped on some days, but they went out regardless of the weather and re-turned several times each day looking like mud wrestlers.

Kiffaney had left them two outfits a day for five days, with the admonition, "Mom I don't want you doing any laundry for the boys." It was a considerate thought, but they had to strip on the back porch after each safari, and their clothes were so muddy I didn't know where to put them other than in the washing machine. They wore gloves and boots of Rick's and mine, and they were having such fun that we couldn't put a damper on it. After they got a few frowns at the store for turning in dirty cans, they also started bringing all dirty bot-tles and cans to our kitchen sink to be washed.

These boys are so different from any kids I reared in that

they were trained at an early age to be very helpful. All three of them can change a tire on a car, put gasoline in the tank, and check and add oil. The Monday after Christmas, while Rick and I lingered at the breakfast table watching the birds at the yard feeders, the boys dismantled the decorations from the Christmas tree, took the tree to the alley, then ran the vacuum and rearranged the furniture in the living room. That more than made up for the muddy clothes I washed for them.

Such a beautiful holiday
November 26, 1981

Thanksgiving is such a beautiful holiday because it causes us all to think of the many things for which we should praise the Lord and give thanks. I like Thanksgiving because it is the one holiday that isn't commercialized by the sellers of gifts but is a pleasant day of being together with friends and loved ones.

At the top of my thankful list this Thanksgiving is the love my husband and I have for each other. I think it's neat that whenever I glance in a mirror or a store window, I see a little old wrinkled granny face, but when Rick looks at me, it's as if he's looking at Miss America 1981. Beauty must indeed be in the eye of the beholder. It's wonderful to know— and it should happen to everyone— that to one other person in this world you're always right, always clever, always believable, always lovable, and always fun to be with.

Second on my list is the wonderful rapport we have with our children. Not that they ever ask our advice, and would nod off to sleep were we to offer them any, but they're such happy, well-adjusted, responsible mates to each other and parents to our grandchildren. We couldn't ask for more.

Third, seldom a day goes by that I don't feel grateful for the wonderful parents I had, who believed in praising the Lord, accentuating the positive, and eliminating the negative. They taught us that it's easier to laugh than to cry, to immediately forget the unpleasant, and to relive and wallow in the pleasant! "Worry" was a dirty word at our house even though nobody reared a big family of children without plenty of happenings that could have dampened spirits. They simply refused to dwell on subjects that were unpleasant. They believed in doing something about a situation if one could, and if one couldn't, forget it and go on about the business of living and enjoying life. Happiness is truly a habit, just as complaining, frowning, feeling slighted, and feeling put upon can be habits, too.

Some questions at Thanksgiving

November 9, 1982

The fact that Thanksgiving is in the next to the last month of the year makes it a fabulous time to sum up and review past months. Are you really doing the things you like to do best? Are you spending time with those you love the most? Do you feel good about yourself and the future? Are you still thinking for yourself, or do you let the TV news people tell you what to think and how to interpret today's news? Do you ever do anything kind for somebody else and keep it to yourself? Do you take care of one of life's greatest gifts, your body? Or do you overeat, oversmoke, overdrink, and underexercise? Do you live each day with so much kindness and consideration for your husband or wife that you wouldn't have to be guilt-stricken about something you've said or done when it's too late?

Do you dwell too much on material things and not enough on nature's beauties? Do you value fast cars, wire wheels, and sun roofs more than you take time to thank God for your wonderful health? Is there someone somewhere whom you've neglected to write who could use an appreciation note from you? Do your husband and children know, by being told again and again, that you love them more than anything else in the world? Do you tell your friends— while they're living— how much they mean to you? Or do you wait until they die, then eulogize them? Do you realize on election day our good fortune to be counted and to have the freedom to say anything we like about any public official? Do you appreciate your good fortune in getting to live in small-town Iowa?

What Christmas means to me

December 22, 1983

Christmas means many different things to different people. Besides causing busy people to pause and reflect on the birthday of baby Jesus, it is the season when people are most filled with love for friends and family. Just as little children thrill with the anticipation of giving and receiving gifts, we oldsters are full of the warmth and happiness that comes to us when we share smiles, companionship, good food, and fellowship with family and dear friends. I've always been disgustingly optimistic to the point where I feel that every week of the year is like Christmas. Here are a few of the things and people who are the Christmas ornaments on my year-round tree.

1. This sleepy little midwestern village where we're so happily settled in for life.
2. Our neighbors so willing to help in any way possible with any project and who share gleefully any piece of good luck that befalls us.
3. The love, companionship, and shared interests that Rick and I have.
4. The fact that Rick and I love and appreciate our in-laws Suzie and Roger as much as we do our children Kiffaney and Courtney.
5. The realization that there's bound to be a period when the grandchildren will outgrow their grandparents— but thank God, it's not this year!
6. Our general good health— the shiniest ornament of all.
7. Sisters— they're wonderful! Rick and I would feel adrift at sea without his sister Mary and my sister Gin! They're appendages of our immediate family unit, to be contacted, consulted, and informed before making any major decisions. They glory so sincerely in all of our good fortune.
8. True friends— God bless them every one. It's such fun knowing people well enough to say anything that pops into your head without their ever taking offense.

For example, I tried to call my friend Maxine Waterman in Mitchellville one Tuesday evening, but she never answered. So I wrote her a letter asking, "Where were you Tuesday night?"

Maxine called me and said, "I was out at Merle Hay shopping center buying a new black purse to go with my new black skirt and my new black sweater."

I replied, "At least I don't need to ask if you're still fat, because I know you are if you're attempting to tuck yourself away in an all-black outfit."

She agreed that I was correct, and just giggled about what I had said.

Another put-down by a dear friend had to do with a bladder-tack surgery I possibly needed. I'm terrified of doctors, hospitals, examinations, and all, and none of my girl friends can understand why I'm so fearful. One of them asked, "Exactly of what are you so frightened?"

My answer was, "Since the surgeon is such a busy gynecologist, I'm afraid he'll mix me up with someone who's having a hysterectomy."

The girls suggested that I mark on my abdomen with a red marking pencil that I wanted a BLADDER TACK ONLY. Then Barb Taenzler added, "And with a tummy the size of yours, you won't even have to write it in shorthand!"

It seems to me that Christmas feelings are those that people have all year— only just a little more so at Christmas time. An ideal Christmas to me is a time when the love of family and friends, the feeling of closeness, appreciation of others' senses of humor, and sensitivity to the dreams and aspirations of friends and family are foremost.

Christmas in Denver
January 10, 1985

Now that both of our children and their families are in Denver, it's the place for us to go at Christmas time. And add my beloved sister Gin and her husband and two of their offspring, including a two-year-old granddaughter. Our brother Don, from Corvallis, Oregon, was with us this year, too.

For the past five years I've tried to promote a firm hand

clasp as a Christmas gift, but nobody listens to me. When Kiffaney was at a sale in Malvern a while back and saw Rick give up on a square black iron skillet that he really wanted, she made up her mind that she'd find him one for Christmas—and she did. Nathan gave Rick a cowbell, and Tyler gave him a compass and digital clock combination for his tractor. Suzie and Courtney gave us a fireplace set for our Franklin stove. We're all crazy about Pat Buckley Moss paintings, and all of the women in the family received those. Kiffaney gave me big gobby yellow earrings for my tent dress, and some lavender ones, too.

I deserve an optimist's award for one of my gifts to Rick. He subscribes to *Fin and Feathers* magazine every year, so I bought him a lifetime subscription. Not until I had sent in the check did I start giving it some thought. If that company knew that the man who had just received a lifetime subscription was going to be seventy years old in May, they would laugh all the way to the bank.

I'm enjoying my two new heads of hair that Santa brought me. One of them has a little coloring in it (not stark white like the rest of my wigs). If people mention anything about the few dark hairs, I'll say it must be from the vitamin B pills I've been taking.

The Three Horse Ranch

A home for the horses

January 19, 1984

This was the big day for Silver, Prince, and Hobo. Their little acreage that Rick has been promising them for years has finally been fenced, the hay moved, electricity and water warmers turned on, and all areas pointed to GO for the horses. It was a very icy day underfoot, to the extent that Rick thought we'd best not try to ride the horses over from Ernie Wederquist's (where they'd been living), so Rick and I led them. To give you an idea of how small the town of Malvern is, it took us only twenty-five minutes to walk the horses from the extreme west end of Malvern to the extreme north end of town.

The horses chose this morning, when the temperature was sixteen degrees above zero, to show extreme intelligence. Usually, when Rick appears with ropes and halters, they make him chase them around for fifteen minutes or so, playing "catch the horses." Not so today. All three halters in hand, he walked up to them, and they just stood there as if they knew that their kindly master finally had their pasture all ready for them.

This is the kind of weather when old folks like us should either be at home cuddled up to the register or be in the sunny South somewhere playing golf and shuffleboard. But this isn't true when we have three such lovable pets as Prince, Silver, and Hobo. It's not that they're that valuable, but we have grown accustomed to them. In fact, had they been more valuable, we might have been able to get rid of them. Rick just knew that anyone who would buy them might send them to the glue factory or the dog food factory, and he couldn't bear the thought. I suggested adopting them out to the best homes applying. I thought about running an ad in the *Leader*, offering to give away three lovable kid-broken horses to anyone who proved they could give them a good home, plenty of food, and loving care. I thought we could interview the people as is done with adoptive parents. Rick said that wouldn't assure us that they'd never sell them. He wants to know that they're loved and cared for as long as they live.

It may sound simple to say that we're going to treat with care three friendly horses until they depart for that great green horse pasture in the sky. And there *is* more to it than that, as I'm learning every day. So far, Rick has said that he'd like to get one of those wild horses from out West, some goats, a couple of steers— and he even asked me if I'd like to learn to milk a cow. He hadn't more than closed the gate on the horses this morning before saying that Ernie Wederquist has a new little colt that he'd surely like to have. To each his own, I always say. Whatever makes him happy!

Rick and I have so many exciting plans for that place. We've ordered 1,000 seedling trees from the state conservation commission. I've already staked off my croquet area and a place for a putting green, and I lie awake nights remodeling that house with bay windows, fireplace, and screened porches.

The afternoon Rick purchased the property, I first had the suspicion that he had only the horses in mind. He said, "The barn is beautiful, with twelve-inch-thick walnut rafters put together with wooden pegs about the size of a broom handle."

I asked, "What's the old house like?"

"I don't know, I didn't go in it," he responded.

"Didn't he have the key with him?" I asked.

"Yes," Rick replied, "I have the key, but I thought you'd want to be with me the first time I went in the house."

Three Horse Ranch

The first picnic at the ranch

March 15, 1984

I haven't minded the cold this winter, and I think the reason is that it hasn't been too icy for my daily walks. By continuing to go out in the below-zero weather, it feels like spring when it gets above forty-three degrees. Once or twice a day I walk down to the Three Horse Ranch. Rick and I had our first-ever picnic there today, a simple but fattening one of ham sandwiches, Waldorf salad, and coffee. So far we don't have any furniture in the old house except a table and five chairs.

After lunch we walked down to the creek, which was frozen and snow-drifted. Rick showed me the well and the well house. It's an eighty-five-foot-deep well that the Bird brothers dug by hand and completely lined with tile. There's a motor that pumps the water for Prince, Silver, and Hobo now, but Rick would like to get the old windmill repaired. That little plot of ground is so exciting to Rick and me that we can scarcely contain ourselves until spring.

Spring at the ranch

July 5, 1984

I forget from year to year how beautiful the flowers are in Iowa in June. The roses are the most gorgeous we've ever had, and Rick lost only five rose bushes last winter. My favorite variety bouquet has roses, daisies, coral bell, gaillardia, and geraniums in it.

One thing that I'm not looking forward to is to bake the hundreds of apple and cherry pies that I do every summer. We're just beginning to run out of last summer's supply. Rick was so pleased when he discovered a Montmorency cherry tree at the ranch.

"Give me a break," I sighed. "There's no way I could bake more cherry pies than I've been baking."

Sometimes I wonder if a rested wife wouldn't be preferable to two freezers full of pies.

Our grandsons at the ranch

July 19, 1984

Our grandsons painted the old farmhouse this week and helped Rick with mowing and weeding, so the old house is beginning to look as if someone lives there. The boys have been riding the horses bareback, and it's nice for them to have the space to ride.

Sunday Rick made a rope swing at the ranch. When he told me he was going to put one up, I asked who would want to swing from a tree, since our youngest grandchild was twelve years old, I found out very soon. That night we went over for a picnic and to ride the horses, all three of the boys and I took turns on the swing all night. Then, lying out on the hill north of the farmhouse, we watched the sky and enjoyed the breeze. We decided to have a wiener roast there the next night, so Bradley and Rick built a place for a bonfire, lined the entire bottom with red tiles, and built a rock wall in a circle around it. Then they made seats from cement blocks and lumber.

The next morning the boys resumed painting the outside of the farmhouse, then went swimming for an hour. After that, we all played golf at Glenwood. About seven o'clock we took our food and went to the farm for the wiener roast. We sat around the campfire and listened on the radio to the Kansas City Royals ballgame. We stayed around the campfire until it started raining.

Tomorrow morning the boys and their dog Arlo will leave by plane for Littleton, Colorado, their new home. They're very excited because their new home is less than six miles from the foothills. Their parents tell them it's the prettiest home they've ever had.

Our grandsons and the dog Arlo all have reservations for the same flight to go to Denver. Their mother told me by phone, "I hate having them all on the same plane."

I suggested, "There are about ten flights a day to Denver, so I can hold one back and put him on a later flight if you like."

Kiffaney had the last thought: "Why don't you just put Arlo on a different flight?"

The farmhouse

December 6, 1984

People get the mistaken idea that I gad about all the time. Not so. The week just past I was either at the farmhouse or at home for six solid days, and I enjoyed every minute of it. We ate lunch at the farmhouse every day. I can scarcely wait for the remodeling to be done so I won't have to carry thermoses and picnic baskets back and forth all the time. We even spent Sunday, from after church until seven o'clock, at the farm. Rick was repairing some things in the barn, and I was putting the prime coat of paint on the outside of the glass doors between the kitchen and the deck.

We're so excited about that kitchen. There's a bay window to the west, and we had planned to put a Franklin fireplace to the right of that. We thought it would be so neat, when it was snowing, to look out the bay window at the snow and have a flaming fireplace to the right of the window. But when we started shopping for Franklins, we discovered that all of the stove companies are into conservation. They're now making stoves without glass windows (the kind you can supposedly fill in the morning and they'll last all day and heat the whole house.) Rick and I went to seven places in Omaha, and the only stove we could find with windows would have taken up about one-third of the bay window view. We had just about decided to get that stove and put it in the corner of the living room instead of in the kitchen. But I wasn't really happy about it, as I wanted light-colored wallpaper in the living room and didn't really want a wood-burning stove in there.

God bless our neighbor Lauraine Breeding. One night when we came home, she was waiting on our back porch with a Sears catalog picturing the exact Franklin fireplace we wanted.

Two other exciting things about that kitchen are the monstrously big porcelain kitchen sink that was in the house originally, plus the stove we've ordered— a "Country Charm" stove from Rogers, Arkansas, which is electric but made to look like an old-fashioned cookstove. Rick thought perhaps we should switch to a new sink, because there's no way for me to have an electric disposal in this old sink, but I'd choose quaint over labor-saving any time.

West end of farmhouse kitchen

Out of commission

February 28, 1985

So much sickness of various kinds is making the rounds, and I had something that slowed me down for several days. I didn't go to a real live doctor because I didn't want to. Our kids, my sister, my high school classmate Hattie Crone, Betty Vinton, and my neighbor Bernice Woodfill all thought I needed to see a doctor. My friends are such fabulous diagnosticians that I didn't need to. Dr. Jane Scherle thought I had gall bladder problems, Dr. Jo Campbell said I had acute indigestion, Dr. Marilyn Burdic said I had an angry colon, Dr. Carol Dean said I had pleurisy, and Dr. Sarah Aistrope thought I had arthritis of the chest muscles. It was a little tougher for Dr. Maxine Waterman of Mitchellville to diagnose long distance, but she kept calling and telling me to take my pneumonia to the hospital.

Rick and I both concluded that whatever I had was brought on by the stripper liquid we were using on the woodwork in the living room at the farmhouse. We had the furnace on and all of the doors and windows closed. We both know better now. Wouldn't it have been terrible if our beloved farmhouse restoration had done me in? The only good part about the ten days I was housebound was how sweet and attentive Rick was. He cooked such good food and left the house only long enough to feed the horses and go to the post office and grocery store.

During the time I was in poor health, I was subjected to jokes stemming from my previous declaration that I intend to leave my body to the medical school in Omaha—which always sends my friends into hoots of laughter and remarks like, "What would the medical school do with that old body?"

One of these comedians said, "I willed my body to science under an assumed name."

Another countered, "I willed my body to science, but science is contesting my will."

Our farmhouse is finished

July 1985

The farmhouse is completely finished, curtained, and furnished— and it's darling. I keep saying that working on it was the most fun I ever had in my life, and Rick keeps saying, "Surely in some of your other lives, before we met, you must have had as much fun!"

This was such a glorious spring weatherwise, and Rick's garden and little orchard and new trees are all doing so well. His garden looked so large to me that I was afraid I might exaggerate the size, so I took the tape measure and measured

The farmhouse

it yesterday so I could get the accurate size. It's 110 feet long and 100 feet wide.

We're eating lettuce, radishes, and onions from it so far and should be picking peas by next week. This is a wonderful year for roses, too.

Brakes and Transmission

December 12, 1985

Rick thinks we're so lucky because Bob Poort approved us as a foster home for two of the kittens that were born in his garage downtown. I had in mind raising them in the barn (that's what Rick said when he first mentioned them) but they have graduated from the barn to Rick's workshop, then to the basement of the farmhouse. It's nice having mousers around a farm, but I also know that each additional living, breathing animal makes it more difficult to get away. The last time we

The barn

left, it took Larry Hedlund to watch the farmhouse, Tom Pearce to tend the horses, and Mary Click to watch our home. Who's going to want to come over to the farmhouse basement daily just to feed our babies if we should want to go away this winter? Besides, Rick wants a dog, some geese, some chickens, and a couple of calves. I hope this retirement doesn't tire us!

But the kittens are adorable. We named the male Brakes and the female Transmission (Missy, for short) because of their being born at Poort's garage.

Snowstorm at the ranch

December 19, 1985

What a beautiful snowstorm we're having today at the Three Horse Ranch! And never a more convenient time for me to be inside, because I've made no plans for Tuesday, Wednesday, or Thursday. By Friday, when I'm planning to play bridge at Vickie Tornquist's, or Saturday night, when we're invited to dinner at Teresa and Bob Buffington's, I might feel pretty snarly about the snow— but today I'm loving it.

Rick has set up a card table in front of the fireplace in the kitchen and has brought a huge box of mail and magazines

8/18/88

from his desk at home. I have five library books with me, and all my unanswered correspondence, a rolled rump roast in the oven, and enough food for the duration of the storm. The view out back through my writing room windows looks like Wyoming or Nebraska— not a building or human to be seen except our huge old gray barn topped by the brass horse weather vane that turns constantly from side to side. Occasionally I can hear a train going by.

The snowdrops look feathery, but they are sticking and piling. It's dark for an early afternoon, so I've turned on our outside Christmas lights and the lights on the balcony Christmas tree to cheer any travelers who have to go somewhere today or tonight.

Actually it snowed quite a lot a week ago Saturday, when Jeff Taenzler and Missy were married, but the roads weren't bad. They had a lovely sitdown dinner for several hundred persons, followed by a dance. I felt all right about the way I was dressed at the time, but for some reason the girls at Duplicate Club Monday all laughed when Carol Dean described my dancing outfit. It consisted of ultrasuede suit, a mink-trimmed hat, and Alaskan dog sled boots. My feet were toasty warm and, besides, it's such fun being eccentric!

Sunday morning it was snowing, but we went to church only to find ourselves locked out. Although it was too stormy for church, the Glenwood Golf Course meeting in Glenwood was well-attended. Rick was elected president for next year.

Wednesday I went to a lovely luncheon at Rena Van Pelt's, north of Glenwood, and came home in a blinding snowstorm. That evening we went to a cocktail party at Janella and Rod Goy's, honoring Governor Branstad. I was surprised at how much younger, shorter, and less sophisticated the governor is in person than he is in his newspaper pictures.

Thursday afternoon Margaret Hageman and I went to a tea at the church. That night Marilyn Burdic and I went to the Nobody's Perfect Club at Jo Campbell's.

Friday I made a steak stew to serve at an early Saturday night supper for seven of my lady friends whom I'd invited for an all-night bridge party at the farmhouse. These were the original Ozarks retreat girls, so I knew they could play bridge endlessly— and we did.

Saturday morning I made a coconut cream pie and a banana cream pie for the church bake sale. Then at noon Rick and I went to the Iowa Department of Revenue Christmas party at the Red Oak Holiday Inn, and afterwards to a lovely party at Dude and Bob Blunt's in Red Oak. Rick and I came home in time to plug in the stew and the coffee pot before my guests arrived. Rick stood out in the snow directing traffic and helping them park.

We didn't quite stay up all night. We went to bed at five o'clock in the morning and were up before eight. Rick picked me up for church, and that was the last wide-awake thing I had to do that day.

Speaking of church and sacrilegious songs, Rick and I heard a ridiculous song on our western music station this morning: "Drop kick me, sweet Jesus, through the goal posts of life!" That's kind of the way I felt the day after the slumber party— as if I'd been drop-kicked through a goal post.

We Travel Some, Too

Don't invite me, if you don't want me

June 24, 1976

Last Tuesday, a little before eight o'clock, I placed a long-distance call to a friend of mine in Washington, Iowa, from whom I hadn't heard for several months.

"What are you up to?" I asked her.

"I'm having forty-eight ladies for a bridge luncheon at the Captain's Table today," she said. "I wish you were here."

· "I'll come," I offered.

Naturally she thought I was jesting. But after I called Rick at his office in Council Bluffs and he okayed the idea and insisted that I drive the "Sunday-only car," the idea started sounding better and better.

This is just another of the many reasons why it's more fun to be a grandmother than a mother. Mothers can't take off on such short notice. There's too much food preparation, arranging for baby-sitters, hauling kids to music and golf lessons, going to pick up little league uniforms or new swimming suits. . . . Then, too, many times during the mother stage, all the clothes allowance goes for the kiddies, so mothers don't have a spiffy outfit ready at a moment's notice in which to face people from the old hometown whom they haven't seen for several years. Also, a mother at that stage doesn't feel she should take gas money that is needed for family swim pool memberships, day camp, and family vacations.

Because I long since gave up on appearing in public with my own straggly hair, I had a choice of two wash-and-wear

Eva Gabor wigs that would make me look like I'd planned this trip for weeks. The only things that didn't point to "go" were my rotten-looking fingernails. Mary Click and Marilyn Burdic both offered to give me quick manicures, but I didn't think I should take the time, so I decided I'd go as I was and talk about our big garden a lot if I noticed that anyone was looking at my nails.

I thoroughly enjoyed driving the Sunday-only car. We'd had it about seven months, and this was only the second time it's been out on a weekday. The trip down there went so fast that it is scarcely worth mentioning. I left Bill Blackburn's station at nine o'clock and was at the luncheon in Washington (thirty miles beyond Iowa City) by two o'clock. At the luncheon one of my old friends generously choked on a sprig of parsley and had to go home, so I even got her tally and got to play bridge. It was wonderful seeing so many of my old friends and those of my mother's who are still living.

That evening I had dinner and indulged in another bridge game at Rachel Jungbluth's. I stayed all night with Elsie Glassburner, and we had breakfast at the North Side Cafe, where I saw lots more people I knew. After visiting several people in the nursing home, I started for Kalona, my birthplace. I dropped in on cousins there, and then went to Sharon Center, where I had lunch with my cousin Paul Stutsman at his beautiful farm. Two other cousins, Dorothy Stutsman and Kathie Berglund, came over to visit with us.

All in all, it was a really fun trip! But I blew it by driving the Toronado. I know I shouldn't have driven the Corvair (Bob and Roger Poort get so tired of coming for me after breakdowns in Council Bluffs and Omaha), but Rick and I have been carefully building up a myth about the Toronado. We keep it in Bertha Angus's garage and take it out only on Sundays. When we get ready to sell it, we will be able to truthfully say that it was owned by a little old couple in their sixties who took it out only on Sundays to drive to church (with the exception of my trip to my hometown!).

The Sunday *Des Moines Register* had a news item about a tornado touching down in Kalona in Johnson County. My neighbor John Click insists that it was spelled incorrectly and that the news item should have said that my Toronado touched down briefly in Kalona in Johnson County. Well, I did have to drive eighty-five and ninety miles an hour to get to that luncheon!

The electrical appliance conspiracy
August 25, 1977

Rick and I held several conferences trying to decide between going on a vacation and staying home and having the house painted or trying to save our falling-off back porch from falling off or putting indoor/outdoor carpet on the front porch. When you're in advanced years, it's a neat cop-out to decide to do whatever is the most exciting and entertaining, because of your age. People should do what they want as long as they're still able to get around. It's advisable to travel while you're able to walk and really see things. It's more pleasant to eat in different places when you're able to eat anything and everything, rather than to wait until you hit the "milk toast" stage in life.

All we needed to do was to discuss a vacation, and our household appliances began to give out one by one. The first to go was the vacuum cleaner, which I had been calling dirty names for a year. That was replaced by a self-propelled vacuum, which for the first two or three pushings I thought was as much fun as a trip to England. Next the dishwasher went. I barely mention that, because I don't mind hand-doing dishes. There will be plenty of time to nag about that after we have our trip. Third in line was the disposal, and I've been substituting trash bags.

Our eleven-year-old self-defrosting refrigerator heard about the game— among the appliances, called "Trying to Worry the Mr. and Mrs. out of a Vacation by Means of a Massive Appliance Breakdown." All of a sudden the water stopped going out of that refrigerator— wherever it had been going out for over a decade— and made a little wading pool in the box under the crispers. I dried it up with several bath towels, trying to avoid calling a repairman.

The latest, and surely the last, blow for the summer was

the demise of the hot water heater, which cracked and leaked all over the basement floor. Rick turned off the water heater, and we're playing "Early-Day Pioneer," or "Cold Water is Better than Hot for Clothes," or "Too Many Hot Baths Dry Out the Skin."

So much for ailing appliances

September 1, 1977

We decided to ignore the needed household repairs in favor of a trip to England and Scotland. For many people overseas trips are like having babies. If you wait until you can afford them, you never have them.

The first time Rick and I went to Scotland, the birthplace of his parents, was in 1973. Besides finding and getting to know an aunt and seven different cousins, we had tea in the Muirhouses farm home where Rick's father was born. Rick's parents came to America from Dundee, Scotland. His father's sister, Flo Smith, still resides in a flat on South Tay Street, where she has lived for forty-five years. We headquartered in a quaint old hotel, The Queens, on the River Tay just a block from Aunt Flo's flat.

On this second trip, one Sunday evening when Rick and I were walking and window shopping in Dundee, a very drunk man walked up to us outside a jewelry store window and started talking to Rick. Rick, who is kind to everyone in this world, visited with the guy like he was an old buddy. When we started to leave, the man held out his hand to shake Rick's hand. Then he wanted to shake mine. I— not being as nice as Rick— decided I didn't want that creep to touch me, so I put both hands behind me and started backing away. Then this fellow, whom I thought was too drunk to know anything, said the best thing in the world he could have said to humble me.

He asked Rick, "Are you taking your mother out for a nice walk?"

Dundee was an excellent place from which to operate, because it's ten miles from Carnousti Golf Club, twelve miles from St. Andrews, and twenty miles from Gleneagles. When we were at Carnousti in 1973, Rick had joined the Carnousti Club, and he has kept in touch with the Scots with whom he golfed. He discovered still another fabulous course on this latest trip, at Oban, on the west coast.

My cousin Neil Shaver had been telling me for years about the high caliber of the London theatre. And I had long been eager to see Buckingham Palace, watch the changing of the guards, view Westminster Abbey, and have dinner at the Savoy Hotel. We were not disappointed.

During the ten days before we left, we had three batches of houseguests, including our niece Marianne Wolf and her family, our niece Linda Stutsman and one of her sons, and my brother Robert Stutsman (a psychiatrist whom I love to try to shock).

We were afraid that by packing hurriedly, we might forget something, but it was much to the contrary, as we ended up shipping back two huge boxes of excess luggage that Rick tired of carrying everywhere. By actual count, we had fifty-three items that we didn't need or want. Among the content of said boxes was all of our dirty clothes, laundry soap, tea bags, money belts, playing cards, a first aid kit, envelopes, black and brown shoe polish, Shaklee's Basic H cleaner, one of Norman Vincent Peale's books, heather, driftwood, two paperweights, six pairs of women's golf socks, four ships carved from bone, London theatre programs, a sketching notebook, three swimming suits, three white dress shirts, a sewing kit, an umbrella, a rain suit, five pairs of hot-weather golf shorts, two boxes of Kleenex, my best Lilli Ann slacks, two jumpsuits, a Mr. Coffee coffee maker and converter, coffee filters, two coffee mugs, two pounds of Butternut coffee, Rick's best ties, and some English and Scottish calendars.

If we're lucky, they'll arrive by Christmas. I have a feeling that for years to come, whenever we can't find something, we'll assume that we lost it in those boxes that we sent uninsured from Oban, Scotland, when we went over in the summer of 1977 to celebrate the Queen's Silver Jubilee. We learned that a person doesn't need a bunch of clothes to travel. Rick, who had taken three suits, wore blue denims to the theatre in London and nobody noticed or cared.

Rick really enjoyed the three musicals and one comedy

that we saw in London this time. The theatre with Rick is kind of like Rick and the game of bridge. He really loves playing bridge, but because he pretends not to like the game, he wins brownie points for playing.

Christmas in the mountains

January 5, 1978

We arrived at Kiffaney and Roger's in Los Alamos, New Mexico, the afternoon of Christmas Eve. This town sits atop the James Mountains, which rise 7,200 feet out of the Pajarito Plateau. They're all that's left of a prehistoric volcano. From Kiffaney and Roger's home they have a breathtaking view of the Sangre de Cristo Mountains. On Christmas Day we took a two-hour walk and watched some fellows rappeling, with the help of ropes, down sheer mountainsides.

The morning after Christmas the three generations of us spent ice skating in a beautiful, wooded setting. Rick was the star of our family ice follies, as he's the only one who dances on ice, skates backward, and makes perfect figure eights.

We spent hours playing a new game, Boggles, in which the contest is to see who can make the most words out of different designated letters. I don't know whether I felt more stupid in the games when nine-year-old Brad did better than I did or in the games when our brainy son-in-law congratulated me on playing a good game (those were games in which he doubled or tripled the scores on me). Naturally we played bridge late every night, and kept a running score.

I never cease to be surprised each Christmas that there's always one gift that's grabbed after by everyone, young and old. The single most popular gift this year was a *Guinness Book of World Records*, which Suzie and Courtney had sent to Bradley. Every time there was a lull in the activities or conversation, someone was reading aloud from that book.

I've known for years how to have enough pillows to go around when there are houseguests, but it's been a while since I've needed to resort to this. Each of my grandsons in Los Alamos had a pillow when he retired hours ahead of the adults, but upon awakening each morning, one or another of the boys had mysteriously lost his head rest. They were good-natured about it and even took to betting about which one would be flat to the bed come the dawn.

The last night we were in Los Alamos, Roger came out of Nate's bedroom doubled over with laughter and asked us to come take a look. That kid had taken his new bicycle chain lock that Auntie Gin and Uncle Herb had given him for Christmas and had locked himself and his pillow together.

In a way, it reminds me of that beautiful old song, "Get Up My Darling Daughter Mabel, We Need the Sheet for the Kitchen Table."

Chained tight

Where was I?

May 20, 1979

Ever since I've known Rick and his family, I've heard about Geneva on the Lake in Ohio, where the family always went for their family summer vacations. They have such fond memories of the place, and Rick had long wanted to take me there. It was natural that this year, when he's retired and we don't have to count vacation days, we would go up to Geneva. I'd heard of Lake Geneva in Switzerland and Lake Geneva in Illinois, and I thought this was just one of the many Lake Genevas.

It is indeed a beautiful lake. In fact, it looked more like an ocean to me. I loved the water and the beaches and the town and the whole bit. Rick was always handing me the binoculars to look way out at the barges and other objects on the water, but I still thought I was on some family-sized lake.

As we were driving home, Rick remarked about how wonderful Lake Erie is.

"I've never seen it," I said.

Rick looked as if I'd stuck an arrow in his heart and asked me, "Where do you think we were all last week?"

"Lake Geneva."

Rick informed me, "Geneva is the name of the town on Lake Erie."

This confession proves many things, but among others, it proves that I don't give a darn where I am— I'll have a good time!

Dear hearts and gentle people

June 10, 1979

Last Memorial Day I said to Rick, "Next Memorial Day I'd like to go to Washington (Iowa) and decorate my parents' graves." Mom died eight years ago, and Dad five years earlier, and I hadn't been back on Memorial Day since. Our family doesn't dwell much on cemeteries and memorials, but more on living full lives, loving a lot and letting each other know it, while we're alive, and expecting to meet again eventually, but not in the cemetery.

We had a marvelous time, which had nothing to do with the fact that it was Memorial Day weekend or that we did indeed decorate Nina and Eli Stutsman's graves. What was exhilarating for me was to be with all of those people who

loved and remembered my parents, and to hear so many
things about them and the rest of my family. It was also fun
to have people recognize me by my mother's face.

We went to a bridge luncheon on Saturday, where I saw
my mother's dearest friends. They are such nice, fun people.
They still miss Mom and enjoyed having me there because I
resemble her in many ways.

Saturday night Rachel and Walt Jungbluth were our
hosts for dinner and bridge. Sunday we had breakfast with
Elsie Glassburner and then went to the cemetery before
church. It was wonderful sitting in our old church in the same
pew and seeing many familiar faces. Naturally we spent some
time Sunday at the Washington Golf and Country Club. I was
seven when they laid out that course, and that's when I
started playing golf.

In between times we called on eight different old friends
of mine. Then, Sunday afternoon, Hazel and Bill Sitler took
Elsie Glassburner and us in their plush Dodge van to Iowa
City to the Hilander for dinner. At nine-thirty we started a
two-table bridge session at Rachel and Walt's. There we saw
special friends Alice and Harold Johnson, Margery Phillips,
and Elsie Glassburner.

We arrived home on Memorial Day about three o'clock,
and not one minute too soon. I had china to wash and
silverware to polish. But that's another story. . . .

Tour guide for the alma mater

November 1, 1979

Carole Shelley Yates, alumni publications editor at the University of Northern Iowa, wrote to me:

Dear Mrs. Smith,

As editor of the UNI *Alumnus* magazine, I'm writing to ask a favor
of you. Many readers comment that they would like to know and see
pictures of the changes on the UNI campus. So I thought that this
year I would do a tour of the campus through the eyes of an alum
who hasn't visited the campus since graduation. I asked Elly Leslie

in the alumni office, and she suggested that you would be on
campus for reunion weekend.

The favor is this—Would you be willing to come to campus on
Friday, October 5th, to help with this article? A photographer and
I would tour the campus with you, and you could point out the
building changes, the way you remember the campus, the memories
you have of different points on the campus. I think it will be a fun
experience, and I hope you'll agree to join me in this adventure. I'll
look forward to hearing from you.

> Cordially,
> CAROLE SHELLEY YATES

I took this letter with me to the Lake of the Ozarks bridge
retreat down at Ione Cook's lake home. I had intended to
answer it in the negative, but Maxine Waterman, my room-
mate down there, and one of my severest critics, asked, "Why
ever *wouldn't* you do it? The one thing you do is photograph
well." Also, my friend Maxine had suggested that I was
probably one of the few remaining mobile members of my
class. Just because Maxine was in about the fourth grade in
1939, she thinks my class members and I are ancient.

As we drove into Cedar Falls, Rick just happened to spot
the university golf course, so he had somewhere to go when
he dropped me off at the alumni office. The editor of the
magazine and the official photographer spent two-and-a-half
hours showing me all around the campus and taking my
picture everywhere. I tried to look nostalgic in front of the old
buildings and awestruck in front of the beautiful new buildings.

I wasn't a BWOC (big woman on campus), active in
dozens of things. I made Kappa Delta Pi (national honorary
in education), was a member of Kappa Pi Beta Alpha (the
organization for students working for bachelor's degrees in
kindergarten-primary education), sang in a trio, and was one
of five Old Gold beauty queens featured in the college
yearbook. Maybe that was why they asked me. Maybe they
were doing a study on whether there is an afterlife for old
college beauty queens!

The alumni office gave me a key-shaped service pin, with
the University of Northern Iowa crest, for acting as chairper-

son of my class reunion and being the greeter. That was an easy job. I seldom had said a word until I was nineteen years old, but when I started talking, I never found out how to shut it off!

The reunion was absolutely fabulous. I recognized people, and they recognized me. On seeing my former classmates, a host of pleasant memories came rushing back. Virginia Shannon West (a Washington, Iowa, friend from the age of five years right through college) was there. Helen Kroeger Lanning, who sang at Rick's and my wedding, was there looking very glamorous. She and Paul Mast were the only two there of the group of ten students who had hitchhiked 100 miles to Washington, Iowa, with me for a weekend at my parents' home. In 1939 I saw nothing unusual about dragging nine extras home with me, and my parents were so gracious that they acted as if I had done them a favor by bringing along my cadre.

When people told me how well I looked, I admitted that it had been no small task and that, if they were to ring my doorbell unexpectedly and see me without makeup, eyelashes, hair, and that darned foundation garment, I'd have to pretend that I was my own mother, or even my grandmother, and say, "I'm sorry, Vera is gone for the day."

A trek westward

April 30, 1981

Rick and I loaded the Mazda and headed for Denver. For the next three weeks we had a perfect vacation—which neither of us needed, as we live such a "do as we please" life anyway. But it really is a battery recharger for us to see our family. Although we keep in fairly close touch, it's nice to be there in person and feel the love and consideration and appreciation of a really close young family unit.

Some things that I think are important are the things that nobody happens to think to say in a letter or on the phone. For instance, the fact that my son Courtney is his daughter's soccer coach thrilled me greatly. I know how hard Courtney works, and it felt good to know that hc and Kristy have three soccer practices and a game together every week. On the night of Kristy's school's talent show, we were pleased to have Courtney give us a guided tour of the school and to be so familiar with every phase of it. Another thing that we hadn't heard by phone was how thrilled they are with their church and minister. He is so interesting according to Courtney, that even when he has preached twenty minutes overtime, Courtney sits there and prays that he won't stop talking!

Ashley and Kristy are so happy and have so many nice girl friends in and out of their house night and day. Kristy is on a gymnastic team and in a ski club and takes dancing lessons and plays soccer. Ashley takes tap dancing lessons and horseback riding lessons and belongs to a ski club. She continues to be so sweet and considerate of her little sister.

Rick and I couldn't imagine that Suzie and Courtney would be going to London for a "five-day weekend," but it made sense after they came back and told us what they had done. They hired a shipping clerk and his station wagon for eight hours on Saturday and eight hours on Sunday to drive them everywhere, and he gave them a sixteen-hour history lesson.

Family reunion

September 2, 1982

Rick, our grandson Tyler, and I checked into the Canterbury Motel in Iowa City on July 30th. It was a delightful place to stay, with a beautiful pool area, whirlpools, sauna, picnic area, the works.

The next morning we picked up Kiffaney (who flew in from South Carolina for our family reunion), and we took her down to Kalona, as I wanted her to see this quaint little town where I was born. It's population is only about 1,300 people. Even so, the area around Kalona is the largest Amish-Mennonite settlement west of the Mississippi River. About 4,000 Amish and Mennonite people are found in the Kalona countryside. We saw farmers using horses (still) in putting up hay. We visited my Grandmother and Grandfather Stutsman's graves at the East Union Mennonite Cemetery.

On the highway between Iowa City and Kalona, we counted ten Amish buggies drawn by horses, and saw several more buggies parked in the town of Kalona. I showed Kiffaney and Tyler and Rick the house where I was born one snowy night in March (delivered by my father, who was a doctor). That's when he made the infamous statement, "It's a nice, fat girl!" Maybe in those days fat was nice.

My parents' courtship and romance sounds like a fairy tale. Dad was a general practitioner in Kalona when Mom was a shy girl who rode into high school in a horse and buggy with her little sister Ethel. Dad was eleven years older than Mother, and they were married the July after she graduated from Kalona High School. After a six-week honeymoon in Colorado Springs they moved into the house where my brothers and I were born (my sister was born in a hospital). We had a live-in housekeeper, Kate Tice, who was there from the day they returned from their honeymoon until my sister was seventeen years old. When Gin and I wanted to get a rise out of Mom, we'd tease her and tell her that we were twelve years old before we realized that Kate wasn't our mother.

Saturday evening Joan and Duane Hills, who live on a beautiful farm just about five miles out of Iowa City, invited all of the out-of-town reunion people to their home for dinner. It was a lovely place, and the food was truly Iowa farm fare, including homemade ice cream. Courtney and Ashley flew in to the Cedar Rapids airport that night. Kristy, my son's ten-year-old, had won first place in three events at a huge swim meet and set a record in her age group, so she didn't want to miss the awards banquet that night. Courtney's wife Suzie stayed with her, and they will drive out to Malvern on Saturday to join the rest of the family.

We had a wonderful time at the reunion at the Paul Stutsman farm. My brother Bob and his wife from Paradise Valley, Arizona, were there. Also there were John Stutsman and his wife and all four of their children plus two daughters-in-law and two grandchildren from Minneapolis, the Lowell Erbs from Wellman, with children and grandchildren, the Duane Hills, Dorothy Tisdale and children from Coralville, and the Eldon Stutsmans, with their remarkable family of six children and many grandchildren. Our granddaughter Ashley couldn't get over how darling all of the children were at this gathering. We had some lively volleyball games and lots of talking, laughing, eating, and picture-taking.

Besides fried chicken and ham and tossed salads and tomatoes, we had baked corn on the cob and potatoes cooked by burying them in the ground. There were at least ten freezers of homemade ice cream. I could hardly decide which was the better between Eldon Stutsman's banana ice cream and his daughter-in-law Ginny's strawberry ice cream, so I kept eating first a dish of one, then a dish of the other. I had my first taste ever of ground cherry pie, made by our host, Paul Stutsman. Delicious! He showed me his ground cherry bushes, too.

Originally, I think, Courtney and Kiffaney had come to the reunion to please their mother, but they really enjoyed themselves. I heard Courtney tell several people that he'd see them at the next reunion. I think he and Kiffaney had the same feeling that I have, when I'm with these cousins— that they're grand people.

Whoever said you can't go back?
September 30, 1982

When Rick and I attempted to register at the Washington, (Iowa) West Motel in my hometown, we were told that our friend Harold Johnson had already signed us in and paid for the room. Two huge "Welcome Rick and Vera" signs were in evidence, and pasted on the mirror was our itinerary for September 1, 1982:

1. Arise! Call 3-2645 for breakfast at Elsie's. Allow 45 minutes for preparation. Directions will be given when you call.
2. 10:00 A.M.: Rick and Johnny to Winga's famous "Coffee Club."
3. Ruth, Vera, Alice, and Elsie: bridge until noon.

4. Noon lunch at the Captain's Table with Vera, Rick, Rachel Jungbluth, Ruth Berdo, Marge Phillips, Hazel and Bill Sitler, Elsie, Alice, and Johnny.

5. Rick and Johnny to preview the Old Threshers' celebration in Mt. Pleasant.

6. Bridge at Johnson's.

7. 3:00 P.M.: High tea for old friends and neighbors at Johnson's.

8. 3 choices for dinner: (1) the Shamrock, (2) Jack Hamilton's Club House, (3) Kalona Town House (Amish food served family style).

Because Elsie had instructed me to call as soon as we arrived, I did, and she asked me if I wanted to play some bridge that night. Silly question! We played at 428 East Main Street. That's the same house where my mom was playing the night she died at the bridge table. Mom would be thrilled to know that one of her kids was playing bridge with Mom's friends. I overbid nearly as badly as my mom did, so her friends may have felt that she had come back!

That clever Rachel Jungbluth presented me with the third scrapbook she's put together using items from my "Grannies Have More Fun" columns. She's been a subscriber since the first year and doesn't miss a thing. Here's a sample page that she wrote, pertaining to Rick's being a rose grower.

**He Didn't Promise Her a Rose Garden
but Everything's Coming up Roses**
by Rachel Negus Jungbluth

Frederick G. Smith, local gardener and award winner, is to be honored this evening at a banquet given by the Malvern Men's Garden Club, "The Summer Knights." Representatives of Jackson Perkins will be on hand to acknowledge the development of several new varieties of roses developed by Mr. Smith and purchased by their company.

The following briefly-described roses will become catalog items available to the public in the near future. Previous to that, however, each will have a chance to become "Rose of the Year," then a collector's item, then a catalog item.

  1. "A Vera is a Vera is a Vera"— a long-stemmed beauty— very colorful!
  2. "Rick's Rose Thistle"— makes a believer of you.
  3. "Stuts"— a later blooming variety.
  4. "Grannie"— the fun rose.

Mr. Smith is also working on a plaid rose— in an experimental stage of development and not perfected at this time. His video game "Atari of Roses" will be on the Christmas market.

Mrs. Smith, who knows the sweet smell of success, enjoys bouquets of beautiful Smith roses in every room in her home. When asked if she helped with the rose garden, she replied, "Whatever for? I'm not a hoe-er, but I do have to hustle to keep the cut roses supplied with water."

All night out with Rick

October 28, 1982

In the wee hours of the morning, Rick and I were breezing along in our Mazda in downtown Omaha. Right beside the new park, everything on the car stopped. The alternator belt was shot. As we were within about five blocks of the Red Lion Hotel, my first suggestion was to walk there, spend the night, and return the next morning to remove the car. Rick quickly vetoed that suggestion by saying that, if we left the car sitting there that night, there'd be nothing left on it by the next morning.

Neatly dressed in a suit, white shirt, and tie, Rick stood beside the car, with hood raised, for more than an hour, and nobody stopped. Nobody cared. Police cruisers, which are usually so plentiful in that area, were apparently on their coffee breaks. I know for sure that I will never again be frightened in that part of Omaha, because we found out that nobody pays any attention to anyone. Lots of cars, trucks, and taxis passed by, and there we sat.

After about an hour-and-a-half, the battery recharged enough so the car started. This time it went about four miles. At that point we were stranded alongside the interstate, with no parking lights on, and the trucks whooshed by about seventy miles an hour, threatening to suck our little car right off the face of the earth. We had passed three different men walking along the highway at that hour of the morning, so I kept expecting one of them to walk up— upon which I would have gone straight up through the ceiling of the Mazda, creating a new sun roof. Rick had a big flashlight on the ready to conk someone on the head if anyone should bother us, but what protection would a flashlight be against a real live gun?

One spurt of the started-up car took us as far as the Bellevue turnoff, and the next spurt put us at the rest stop by three o'clock in the morning. Besides places to freshen up, rest stops also have telephones. I was filled with great ideas. Jo Campbell is a light sleeper and has five extra bedrooms. Marilyn Burdic is a light sleeper and would have come for us. Our neighbors the Clicks also would have driven over. Don Aistrope would have done the same. Our friend Betty Vinton lives only about five miles from there, and she would have come over if we had called her. On top of all that, Rick has belonged to the Triple A Club for thirty years and has called only once.

Usually it's advantageous to live in a small town and know all the facts about the people with whom you do business. This wasn't one of those times. Rick wanted his very own garage owner to come, but since he's a single parent with three small children, Rick didn't want to call him until morning. We knew that the garage owner's father (and partner in the business) and his wife were visiting a daughter in Kentucky, so they couldn't be called upon to baby-sit their grandchildren in the wee hours.

Rick told me that I was free to call anyone for a ride and go on home, but he refused to vacate his third worst car. I knew that I couldn't rest anywhere while Rick was sitting at that rest stop, so I resigned myself to our fate. The seats in the Mazda recline, and Rick had a blanket in the trunk, so we

settled down to wait for the dawn or the ax murderers—
whichever came first.

When I realized that I couldn't persuade Rick to do anything or go anywhere without his car, I turned to God. I'd
heard that he watches over children and old folks, so I placed
us in his care and went to sleep. When I told Rick the next day
how frightened I had been that night, he said, "I could tell. It
took you almost two minutes, after you lay down, before you
were snoring."

California here we come

April, 1984

It had been nine months since we'd seen Kiffaney— the
longest time I've ever gone without seeing her. Rick didn't
want to fly, and I didn't want to drive, so we compromised and
went on Amtrak.

A few of the things that made our visit so enjoyable were:

1. Basking in the sun on the patio.
2. Picking oranges, lemons, and grapefruit, as well as
flowers, in the yard in March.
3. Going to Bradley's two band concerts. One was with
the marching band, and the other was a pops concert in the
school auditorium.
4. Going to Nate's and Tyler's soccer games.
5. Attending the awards day at the twins' junior high,
where Tyler was named outstanding student by two different
teachers.
6. Going to the nearest McDonald's and watching Bradley do his clean-up chores at work.
7. Being part of the excitement and confusion of the ten
or twelve phone calls that Nathan received each night.
8. Being included in the many bridge games.
9. Being there when Kiffaney entertained her book club.
10. Taking side trips to Santa Cruz, and the seventeen-
mile drive along the ocean to Monterey and Carmel. Rick and

I browsed the shops in Carmel, then spent the afternoon on the sandy, sunny beach. Back in Monterey, we went to Cannery Row and had fish dinners at the Bullwhackers' Cafe.

11. Reading Bradley's high school newspaper. First I found him listed with the sophomores who had perfect grade points. And in a story in which teachers had been asked to name an outstanding student, Bradley Frank's name was second on the list of sixteen students. I thought that was remarkable, as he had been in that school only since last fall and there were 1,400 students from which to choose.

Two trips to Colorado

October 18, 1984

Fortunately we were traveling in the pickup in Colorado, because daughter-in-law Suzie gave us three pieces of furniture— a platform rocker, a chest of drawers, and a beautiful oak refractory table— for our farmhouse. Courtney took Rick golfing at Heather Ridge Country Club, and Suzie and I went shopping in Courtney's red Mercedes convertible.

We divided our week into thirds, to visit my sister as well as both children. My daughter's family was last because Bradley had a band program in which he played a French horn solo then did a jazz dance with a female partner and five other couples. The twins razzed him unmercifully because Bradley doesn't date and has no apparent interest in girls. His rotten little brothers kept saying to him afterward, "Bradley touched a girl!"

Granny had goosebumps and a few tears when Bradley played his French horn solo perfectly. He did much better than his granny had done on the bassoon when she forgot her piece completely while competing in the finals of the state music contest forty-nine years ago. At our class reunion, two of my classmates reminded me of that fiasco. Can you imagine remembering something like that for fifty years? I still remember the darling new dress I had for the contest— navy and white silk polka dots with a white collar and a red bow tie. I was well turned out for my big floppo!

On Saturday morning Nathan and Tyler both had soccer games at fields about twenty-five miles apart. We watched about fifteen minutes of Nate's (which turned out to be a 1–1 tie), then tore over to Ft. Logan to see Tyler make the only goal by either team that day.

We've always taken two or three days to drive between Denver and Iowa, but we were anxious to see what progress had been made at the farmhouse. We hit the driveway at two o'clock in the morning and inspected it as much as possible by flashlight. W. and W. Construction had been busy while we were gone. The bay window, glass doors, and other windows were all in, both bathrooms in working condition, and decks built the entire length of the kitchen and clear across the west end of the house. We were so excited that we unloaded the entire pickup and unpacked everything and didn't go to bed until four o'clock.

Rick was afraid that, after all of the beautiful scenery in Colorado, we might not be so stuck on our view west overlooking the open countryside. But that view is still the prettiest one anywhere to me.

I'll be flying back to Denver next Thursday for the "hard body" invitational gold tourney at Heather Ridge Country Club. Our daughter-in-law and two of her friends have been hosting this event for four years now and are into improving their bodies and their general health. They invite about sixty ladies, who all come in costumes. When we were in Denver last week, I rented an old-fashioned bathing beauty's outfit (complete with pantaloons), a night-cap style cap, black tennies, and a sand bucket. The invitations were in the shape of pigs. The mayor of Aurora will be driving the drinks cart this year, and they'll have a parade in the parking lot, at which a lady will be crowned queen. I'll be gone only four days this time. Life is such fun and so full of choices. What dummy ever said, "Your school days are your happiest days?"

A Canadian trip with Bradley

November 14, 1985

It was Indian summer everywhere, and it rained only two days in three weeks. Rick and Bradley and I first went up to northern Canada to the town of Hailebury, where Rick and his family had to flee from a forest fire and spent two days on Lake Timiskaming to keep from being burned alive. They lost everything and went by a Salvation Army train to Toronto, where the Salvation Army fed and clothed them and gave them shelter until Rick's father secured a job at T. Eaton and Co. Rick's parents had three young children, and it must have been terrifying.

The province of Ontario is beautiful country. We loved Ottawa and the parliamentary buildings there.

Today we received the following letter from our grandson (age seventeen), who had accompanied us on the trip:

Dear Grandma and Grandpa,

Thank you, thank you, thank you for including me in your plans to take such a marvelous trip! I can never tell you how grateful I am to have been able to experience such an outing, and what an outing it was! Just think— we traveled over 3,000 miles through the farms and beautiful woods and hills of the Great Lakes area and Ontario. We stretched clear across to the Massachusetts seashore, experiencing beauties of nature every bit of the way. Our stay in peaceful and sunny Massachusetts and then on into Niagara Falls was really something! I really did have a once-in-a-lifetime, great time over those 3,000 miles, eating in all those restaurants, staying in all those motels, hotels, inns, and even Mary's house, and of course seeing the sights. I am truly thankful that I had a chance to do such a thing, and, again I sincerely thank you.

Last Saturday Dad and I spent the day together at the state volleyball tournament in Colorado Springs. We had a great time, and I got to drive the Honda there and back! I told Dad that you looked kind of sad when I left, Grandpa, and I thought this might be so because you never had any kids of your own. Dad asked me if I thought you knew that I think of you as my real Grandpa, and I said "yes," but I thought it wouldn't hurt to tell you, to be sure. Indeed, Grandpa, you are the only real Grandpa I have ever known and spent a lot of enjoyable time with. I never knew Grandma's first husband, and never really got to know Dad's dad. You are my one and only true Grandpa, and a better Grandpa I don't think I could find. Yes, you are the Grandpa in my heart and mind, even though you didn't raise my mom. It just doesn't matter to me. I love you, Grandpa.

Sincerely,
BRAD

P.S. I'm not forgetting you, too Grandma. You're my one and only real Grandma, and I love you too! See you guys this Christmas! Bye!

Some Memories of
Old Friends

I'd do it all over again!

June 7, 1979

Yesterday I had one of the most fun parties I've ever had. Barbara Newman of Carson, California, who is visiting her daughter Leslie Speck, over Mineola way, consented to entertain at our organ. And can she ever entertain! This was a great opportunity for us to invite good neighbors who are non-bridge players— Virginia Primrose, Lauraine Breeding, Maud Wilson, Bernice Woodfill, Bertha Angus, Winnie Myers, Ruth Adkins, Frances Thaller, Ruth Bloedel, and Jo Poort.

Barbara's music was so thrilling that we couldn't sit or stand still, and it was impossible to keep from humming and singing along while she played. The second hour turned into a regular sing-along fest. We dedicated the song "Mary Lou" to Mary Lou Wearin of Hastings and the song "Margie" to Marjorie Dashner of Glenwood, and we sang about 100 other songs. Vicki Tornquist, Jacque Mulholland, and Bonnie Pierce suggested that we should have typed out words to some of the music that was popular before their time. Joanna Perkins, who is also very young, said that she knew the words to all of those songs from hearing her mother sing them. Zelma Wortman and Arwanna Hansen said they could scarcely enjoy the music for thinking how their husbands would have loved hearing Barbara play.

Two ordinarily quite proper and sedate ladies couldn't resist the urge to stay after the invited time was over. Fay Benton sat quietly on the porch to listen to more music. Our neighbor Lauraine Breeding left very formally, then went around the house and came in the back door, hoping we wouldn't notice her bright yellow suit again, or hear her when she belted out the great songs of the thirties and forties.

Barbara loves playing so much that she sat and played more after the guests had left. We sat on the porch a while, and then Leslie, Barb, and I snacked on some of the 121 ham balls I had put in the freezer the last time Corky had a sale of ground ham. They left at three thirty. By eight-thirty I'd returned the chairs to the community building and finished doing dishes and putting them away. Rick was playing in his Glenwood golf league.

Rick asked me, "Are you glad your party's over?"

I said, "Heck no—I'd love having one just like it tomorrow."

My only regret was that Jo Campbell, Barb Taenzler, and Leslie Speck were stuck in the kitchen until after the second group had been served. Next time I have a party, I'll leave only monotones in the kitchen.

Uncle Joe Shaver

March 12, 1981

When I returned from the post office on Monday afternoon, Rick greeted me with, "I have some bad news for you, Honey." He told me that my cousin Neil Shaver had called and said that Uncle Joe Shaver had died. I said, "That's not bad news—that's wonderful. I'm so happy for Uncle Joe."

I'm not as heartless as that may sound, but I had seen this once dynamic man, full of enthusiasm, go downhill this past year into someone who told us every time we visited him that it's hell to get old. He'd lost his eyesight and his sense of balance, and the last few times we visited, he had to ask us who we were. He couldn't even remember that I was the daughter of his once so beloved sister Nina.

Uncle Joe tried to look and act tough, but he was an old softie underneath it all and liked best the people who stood up to him. He had had a fascinating life that embraced many occupations and hobbies.

In the early days of his marriage, he was a hog farmer at Kalona, Iowa, and an auctioneer. When I was a young girl in Washington, Iowa, Uncle Joe was in the construction business in Omaha. When I was about ten years old, Mom and my aunts Hettie and Ethel and cousin Charles Ives and I made a trip by car to visit his family. It took us all day to drive from Iowa City to Omaha over dirty, rutty roads. The Shavers lived in a beautiful home that Uncle Joe had built. My cousin Elmo had a movie theater in the basement and charged the neighbor kids five cents for admission. He had an organ down there and played music that was appropriate to whatever was happening on the silent screen. Shortly after that the Shavers moved to Los Angeles, where Uncle Joe was in the real estate and insurance business.

After Uncle Joe was sixty years old, he moved back to Omaha, where he had one-half interest in a grocery store. He then bought out his partner and enlarged the business to nineteen stores.

Uncle Joe was crazy about horses, particularly race horses, and had a stable of nineteen in Florida for many years. He raced horses at Ak-Sar-Ben for about ten years and lived for his early morning racing form.

About four years ago, when Jo Campbell and I were enroute to the Cornhusker Bridge center in Omaha, we stopped at Uncle Joe's office. When we were admitted, there sat Uncle Joe with his shoes off, enjoying some peanuts and a cocktail with his pretty blonde secretary at about eleven-thirty in the morning. After a few minutes of exchanging pleasantries, he said, "I hate to do this, but you gals will have to get out, because I haven't picked my bets for today yet." This was a 90-year-old man speaking!

Everything started downhill when Uncle Joe began to lose his eyesight and couldn't drive anymore. Then his eyes got so bad that he couldn't read the racing form or watch TV. The last year of his life Uncle Joe spent in the Bethany Lutheran Nursing home in Council Bluffs. He still had several things going for him in that he never had a pain and he had an excellent appetite right up to the end, when his heart gave out.

Bad news that Uncle Joe died? Phooey! That's the best thing that's happened this week. And I really loved you, Uncle Joe. . . .

My friend Maxine Waterman (it is she)

March 24, 1982

Although Maxine Waterman and I have had a mutual admiration society for some fifteen years, we delight in slamming each other. We met when my husband and I first moved to Glenwood and were sitting on the bench in the hall in the courthouse basement waiting to take our driver's tests. Maxine, who was a secretary at social services, saw us sitting there and came up and introduced herself.

Maxine and I are alike in many ways, the most important of which are that we both have lots of guts and more than enough self-confidence to share with a dozen or more other persons. Because we're like this, we have tried to help each other to become more humble—which is no easy task. Each of us claims that the other is jealous of her. I maintain that Maxine is jealous of me because of my slim legs and hips. Maxine claims that I am jealous of her because it doesn't look as if she's concealing a basketball under her skirt front. I maintain that Maxine (who is crazy about kids) is jealous of me because we have five wonderful grandchildren. Maxine maintains that I am jealous of her because she has real, live thick, manageable hair growing out of the top of her head, rather than being reduced to wearing wigs like I do.

It's doubtful if I've ever corrected anyone else's grammar (outside of the classroom) in my life. I think it's rude, rotten and unnecessary to do to anybody. When we were in Mitchellville over Thanksgiving, I noticed that Maxine was saying when answering the phone, "This is her" or "This is me" instead of "This is I" or "This is she."

When I called this to Maxine's attention, she said, "I've said that all my life."

I retorted, "I'll bet you did—coming from Hazard, Kentucky."

We had a big grammar exchange on using the predicate nominative. Eventually I ended up by suggesting that she forget the whole thing and simply answer the phone by saying, "Maxine Waterman speaking" and just be thankful that her phone rings often!

The Buffingtons' third daughter marries
August 2, 1979

Teresa Buffington had what could be likened to a storybook romance and marriage. She and Bob are living happily ever after. When Teresa was seventeen years old and living in Montevideo, Uruguay, with her family, Bob Buffington went to Montevideo on a trip. Teresa and Bob were introduced by a mutual friend from California, and they dated for about eight months. Bob returned to the States and asked Teresa to come to Glenwood, Iowa, to marry him. Teresa's parents wouldn't let her leave the country without being married first, so it was decided that they would be married by phone. The Percibals had a wedding and reception for Teresa. An uncle stood in as a proxy for Bob and the vows were exchanged by phone.

Teresa said that, when their children look at the pictures of her wedding and reception and ask, "Where's Dad?" she always says, "Every time something important comes up, Bob's busy with his farm work."

This little seventeen-year-old city girl from South America (whose family had servants and she had never turned a hand at home) came to a strange country six miles out of a small Iowa town to a huge fifteen-room house, where she was the cook, maid, laundress, and lawn boy.

Teresa must be this world's most adaptable person. She has taken to everything about the farm— even to pulling baby calves in the middle of the night. Teresa has raised chickens, has a huge garden, freezes and cans, mows their seven-acre lawn with a riding mower, refinishes furniture and antiques, paints, is a super cook and hostess, has reared four beautiful and helpful children, and is gorgeous looking and a fun person to be with. One of my most prized possessions is a winter scene picture of a barn that Teresa painted and gave me.

Her daughter, Kathy Ann Buffington, and Hysler Cody Runyan III were married in the Baptist Church in Glenwood on Saturday afternoon. Kathy was beautiful and was preceded down the aisle by her two sisters, as well as two of Kathy's school friends. Kathy graduated from the University of Wyoming this spring with a degree in business, and her husband is a senior law student at the same university.

Two funny incidents come to mind whenever I think of Kathy. The first was when she first started college and chose to go to one in Texas because she thought she wanted a warm winter climate. But she was homesick and lonesome and too far from home, and she kept calling her mother, lamenting that she didn't know anyone and had no friends. Teresa said, "I finally told her that it's hard to make friends with one ear attached to the telephone receiver. Get out of the phone booth and look around."

In the other incident, Kathy was holding down the farm all by herself. She glanced toward the end of their long lane and saw a car parked there. It made her nervous, and the more she watched and nothing happened, the more nervous she became. Finally she loaded the shotgun and started down the lane. She isn't five feet tall and probably weighs about ninety-five pounds dripping wet. When she reached the bottom of the lane, she discovered that the troublesome car was her own— which she had parked in front of the house without putting it in "park." It had taken itself down the hill.

Jefferson claims Dr. George Gallup
August 28, 1980

Last Sunday the *Des Moines Register* carried an interesting story about Dr. George Gallup, of the famous Gallup poll, and gave an account of his return to his hometown of Jefferson, Iowa, for a celebration. I felt disappointed to read nothing more about it than the name of his wife of many years, Ophelia. Ophelia Miller Gallup, her sister Barbara, and their parents, Mr. and Mrs. Alex Miller, were our nextdoor neighbors on South Marion Avenue in Washington. Mr. Miller was editor of one of our two newspapers, and Mrs. Miller was Secretary of the State of Iowa. Mrs. Miller was the instigator of the Iowa Highway Patrol system, which first issued drivers' licenses in Iowa.

Yes, folks, I know I've been living a long time when I realize that I was about fifteen years old before anyone in this state had to have a license to operate an autombile. At that time, anyone of any age and any capability was entitled to drive a car, and I learned to drive when I was eleven. My dad let me take his big old Buick to school on my birthday when I was in eighth grade, and I loaded it with friends and stripped the gears on Main Street.

There were no stop signs in those days either. All of us were on our own. But there were fewer cars than there are now.

Locating an old friend
November 15, 1980

I noticed in the *Leader* that a lecture on attracting wild birds is to be given next Tuesday evening in Glenwood by a Dr. Robert Moorman of Ames. His wife, the former Ruth Wasson of Blairsburg, was one of the six bridesmaids at my wedding in 1941. I called them and invited them to come to our house for dinner before the lecture. Will that ever be fun after so many years! Ruth and I taught together in La Porte City, Iowa, and I knew and loved all of her family.

Ruth said that her eighty-one-year-old mother is still driving, and she had driven to their house for Thanksgiving. Ruth said that she and her mother had discussed me yesterday and were wondering what had happened to me. We'll have trouble covering those thirty-nine years in a few hours!

P.S. I had forgotten that Ruth was a home economics major. I'll either clean house on Monday or take comfort in the little saying that Maxine has on her refrigerator door: "Dull people have immaculate houses."

Please eat and run!

November 13, 1980

When we moved to the Glenwood area fourteen years ago this Thanksgiving, the first people I met were Irene McMannigal, Ardeth McLaughlin, Peggy Buffington, and Maxine Waterman. We formed an instant and permanent admiration society.

Maxine's husband was the minister of the Methodist Church, and the parsonage was right next door. Maxine issued a standing invitation for us to have dinner with them every Sunday twenty minutes after church let out. There was only one condition attached to this generous invitation. You're probably guessing things like:

1. Doing seven weeks' back ironing.
2. Giving our old clothes for the missionary box.
3. Singing in the choir.
4. Washing the windows at the parsonage.
5. Memorizing the books of the Bible.
6. Chairmaning the fellowship dinners at the church.
7. Scrubbing the kitchen floor.
8. Going to church camp.

No, it was none of the above. The only thing Maxine wanted was our solemn oath to leave their premises the minute dinner was over so she would be free to run upstairs and take her beauty nap!

Let's hear it for Marilyn Burdic

March 10, 1976

Several weeks ago on an early Thursday morn, seven Mills County housewives were bestirring themselves and dressing for a trip to the Eppley airport. They went up to wave and shout goodbye to the Allen Burdic family and Karen Kruse, who were departing for Hawaii. These ladies are members of Mrs. Burdic's beatnik bridge club, lovingly known as the Nobody's Perfect Club.

When Rick asked why we felt we had to go up there at that hour to wave goodbye, I didn't have any snappy answers. I began to think about it and decided to jot down some of the reasons why.

On first meeting Marilyn, she might appear to be an ordinary woman, in her early thirties, with a devoted and successful husband and two handsome, healthy, smart, and friendly children. The part about Marilyn that is far from ordinary is the real compassion she feels for people. She identifies with a wide variety of personalities and situations. She truly cares about people, and they care about her.

I dare to say she could win honors for maximum number of hours of volunteer work in the community, in spite of the fact that she's the original "Mrs. Clean" with her own housework. She's always right there for visual testing at school, band mothers' club activities, Friends of the Library benefits, volunteer book-mending sessions, typing for the Bloodmobile, nursery school benefits, and publicity chairwoman every year for the Malvern performance of the *Messiah*. She has fed, single-handedly, all of the musicians coming from Omaha to enhance the Messiah program.

Marilyn's talents include her ability to play both piano and organ beautifully. She plays by ear and is a talented musician. She could be a stand-up comedienne— far funnier than Joan Rivers and other entertainers on the boob tube. Nothing that happens to her or hers is a dismal happening but, rather, a case for hysteria in the telling.

A dream of a daughter, Marilyn sees her mother at least twice a week and calls her in between. Her mother is a riot, too. It's fun being with them, as their patter is similar to the type you used to hear in vaudeville. They draw their material from the good old days when their family (which numbered eleven children) lived, loved, laughed, and were happy in a one-bathroom house. The fact that Marilyn's present home has three tiled bathrooms for their family of four could have gone to her head, but it hasn't. In spite of many talents and sterling qualities, she isn't the least conceited. And Marilyn never tries to put anyone down or act superior.

Because of one of Marilyn's characteristics, I sort of hate her. It's her size five figure that bothers me. She eats more calories intentionally in one day than I eat accidentally in a year, and she still remains proportioned like a clothes model!

Another wonderful friend

July 14, 1983

Everybody knows I'm a tough old bird whose tear ducts are practically never used, but I cried this morning. In the morning mail we received the most beautiful afghan I've ever seen— off-white, with squares of yarn-embroidered violets put together by crocheted yarn borders about five inches wide. It was made for us by a dear, eighty-nine-year-old friend in Denver by the name of Maud Etheridge. Our friendship goes back lots of years to 1949.

When we moved to Newport Street in Denver, our nextdoor neighbors were an army sergeant, his English-born bride, their two children, and his mother-in-law, Maud Etheridge. Maud's husband had died of a concussion after a bomb was dropped on their home in London.

Shortly after we moved to Denver, my husband's mother (who had lived in the Chicago area) became ill, needed surgery, and came to the Denver area to be with us. My mother-in-law, Mabel, and the neighbor's mother-in-law, Maud, became good friends.

My husband Courtney asked them one day, "If I buy you two old dragons a house, would you like to live together?"

They were overjoyed, so he bought them a cozy, two-bedroom, brick home just one block from us, and they lived there happily together for years until Mabel died. Meanwhile, Maud's family had been transferred to South America, then to England, but Maud stayed on in Denver. Maud and Mabel were our dinner guests every Sunday and every holiday, and Maud was like a third grandmother to our children. I didn't learn to make decent gravy for sixteen years because Maud always came to the kitchen and made it for me.

I'll never forget the gorgeous outfits Maud made Kiffaney and me when Kiffaney was five years old. Kiffaney's outfit consisted of lavender knitted pants and a matching lavender sweater edged in white angora. And Maud made a tam, mittens, and scarf of the same lavender yarn. For me she made a full-length knitted lavender coat and matching tam. That was about as conspicuous an outfit as I've ever had. I loved it!

Maud is one of the dearest persons who has ever touched my life, and she and her daughter Doris were two of the biggest reasons I was dying to see London. They had told us so much about it. When we went to England, we looked up several of Maud's relatives, and they were charming, too.

Dear John

October 10, 1985

We're still missing John— the best neighbor we ever had. There should be a law requiring permission from elderly neighbors before someone they love and depend on is allowed to move away.

In 1970 we got the greatest extension to our family that anyone could ever ask, in Mary, John, Tracy, and Andy Click. They moved to Lincoln Avenue when Tracy was in first grade. We went every step of the way with her while she took piano and flute lessons, learned to swim, learned to ski, went two years to college, and obtained a fine job in computers at Mutual of Omaha. Andy is finishing high school this year. He has become so much more mature and less bashful that it's not even fun to tease him anymore.

Mary has always been like a daughter to me. In fact, she remarked the first time we met, "You're older than my mom!" We've borrowed everything from each other from sugar and vinegar to clothing and vacuum cleaners. Before Mary started working, we lunched together about three times a week. I could call on her for everything (just as I could another neighbor, Lauraine Breeding), and they'd give me anything they owned. And speaking of good dispositions— during the sixteen years of living by Mary and Lauraine I never knew either of them (or me) to be "down." Now that's some kind of record!

But to get back to our man John— one of the friendliest, most accommodating, sincere men I've ever known— it became a habit for us to call on him during any crisis or near crisis, and he always gave us the feeling that it was a privilege for him to lend a hand. He had so many smarts about everything from gardening to car repairs to appliance repairs to just general knowledge. I even liked John's jokes fresh from the packing plant.

About a year ago, John (a U.S. government meat inspector) applied for a promotion in Greenfield, Ohio. He received word about the same time that Swifts announced its closing in Glenwood that he could have the job in Ohio.

We're glad that John got the promotion. He likes the job, he likes the town, and he has already made nice friends there. But we hate having him gone.

Remembering more old friends
December 26, 1985

This Christmas season I've been thinking a lot about old friends. In the past year we were visited by a former childhood playmate and neighbor, and I've visited two other friends from that same neighborhood on South Fourth Avenue in Washington, Iowa.

It seems strange that a person can go over fifty years without seeing someone, then feel as comfortable with that person as if it had been yesterday. Millie Lemley Schoemaker had lived in Aruba many years, then in Texas. Two weeks before her fiftieth high school class reunion, she moved back to Washington, bag and baggage, without having even visited there for thirty-five years. She attended a luncheon given in my honor when I went back the next year for my reunion, then entertained us in her home. She really made a difference in Washington. The first week back, she heard that the beautiful old Milwaukee depot was going to be demolished. Millie sent a personal check to the main office of the railroad to save the depot, then proceeded to interest others in being financially responsible.

Millie is very interested in antiques and art and is much more attractive at this age than I remembered her as a young girl. Millie is one of my few friends who never had any children and is glad she didn't, but we have other things in common.

Another neighbor of ours, from the time I was two years old until I started junior high, is Donna Clow, who lives in Carver, Massachusetts. On our trip last month, we spent a day with Donna and her sister and brother-in-law and taught them the game "Spite and Malice." Today we received a letter from Donna's sister, Doris, in which she wrote:

"I nearly sent you a telegram saying, "Don't have time to write— too busy playing "Spite and Malice." Your little card game has so cut into my everyday activities that it's a disgrace. Donna Taylor and I have played until after three in the morning, and Donna Clow and I play constantly. Daughter Donna stayed home from work one day to rake leaves, and she called for me to come up so we could play during her rest periods! She did get her front yard done, but that was all.

We were all very much impressed by Bradley when you visited here. We were also delighted to get acquainted with Rick and enjoyed him very much— particularly his horse stories. I could listen to animal stories all day.

Donna Taylor will be down tomorrow for some leftover turkey— and perhaps a little "Spite and Malice."

Love,
DORIS

In unpacking Christmas decorations this week I came across a chubby, jolly, ceramic Santa Claus that I had won as a bridge prize years ago in Denver. The lady who painted Santa is another dear friend, a schoolmate from sixth through twelfth grades, then a member of two of my bridge clubs in Denver for twenty-five years, Wilma Palmer Febinger.

Wilma and I did many things together, such as running the nursery on Sundays at the Park Hill Methodist Church, going to young mothers' classes at the YWCA to learn how to make flower arrangements, and book reviewing at the Emily Griffith Opportunity School. It was Wilma's idea to go to some rug-braiding classes, but I was the one who loved that and ended up making eleven full-sized rugs in three years. I hadn't intended to part with any of them, but when we were having problems selling a house that was overbuilt for the neighborhood, a man came along and said he'd buy the house if we would leave the rugs. My husband thought we shouldn't leave the rugs, but I was so anxious to make the sale that I would have left the children had they asked for them!

We went back and forth for dinner and bridge with the Febingers for years. We always took our children and wished they could be good friends. I don't think they could ever stand each other!

Billie Hines

September 22, 1986

The old friend who has been in my mind constantly of late is Billie Hines. She's one of those persons with whom one feels immediately comfortable and warm. I met her thirty-five years ago when Courtney was in first grade. Billie's daughter Linda was in Courtney's class at Graland Country Day School, a private school about five miles from our home. Linda had missed school, and Billie wanted to get her assignments so Linda could make up the work at home. Billie looked on the pupils' list for an address near where they lived so she wouldn't have to drive too far to get the book or the assignment.

She rang our doorbell at five o'clock— a complete stranger to me before then— and came in. We were still visiting sixty miles a minute two hours later when the phone rang. It was her husband, calling to see how long ago she had left and thinking she must have been in an accident.

Billie became one of my best friends and joined our ladies' bridge club and our couples' club, and we wasted many happy hours together shopping and dawdling over coffee. She had the best disposition in the world and is such fun!

I remember the year that I had my twenty-year high school class reunion. That was the same year that Billie's husband Bill had his class reunion in Kenesaw, Nebraska.

Bill, a brilliant, well-known doctor, probably was one of Kenesaw's most successful graduates. We were all anxious to make a good impression on the home folks but were all pressed for surplus cash to pay for everything it involved. Our reunions were only a month apart, so Billie and I bought a beautiful blue dress together. We split the cost of matching blue pumps, a merry widow bra that nipped us in at the waist and built us out where it is popular to be thus, and even bought earrings and necklace jointly. I can still see that beautiful blue brocade princess-style dress that cost all of thirty-five dollars—which we thought was astronomical at the time.

I can't remember anything wonderful that I ever did for Billie, but I remember that she and Bill furnished all of the champagne for Suzie and Courtney's wedding reception. And when Rick and I were married, Billie came out from Denver with all the rest of my old bridge club. I never saw her after that. Last month Billie died of lung cancer. You were one of my favorites, Billie. I loved you.

An antique friend

January 2, 1986

Seven ornaments on the Christmas tree in the kitchen at the farmhouse remind me of my friend Clarky White. Clarky was my across-the-street neighbor in Denver for ten years, and she belongs to the Colorado group that still plays bridge in the mountains once a year.

Clarky's husband had a Chevrolet dealership in Lakewood, Colorado, and he gave her a new Corvette convertible each time the new models came out. One time, after Clarky had had eye surgery and wasn't allowed to drive, we went clear to Montgomery City, Missouri, for an antique auction, via Clarky's yellow Sting Ray, with me at the wheel. One of the restaurants where we ate along the way had some beautiful hand-painted ceramic Christmas tree ornaments in shapes of gingerbread men, snowmen, different animals, and ones that looked like cookies. They were so different, and Clarky and I fairly knocked each other down getting a supply to take home with us for the next Christmas. We had never seen ones like this in or around Denver. The next Christmas, when I was unwrapping these priceless gems, I happened to turn over one of them. On the back it said, "Made in Loveland, Colorado."

Clarky and I went on many antique forays together and had a ridiculous habit of hiding our purchases in each other's homes. One time we went to a sale, and Clarky bought a dough bin and I bought a darling iron stove. Clarky put her dough bin in the master bedroom at our house, and I put my stove in the Whites' garage. The next week or so my folks came out for a visit. My husband said to my dad, "Doc, I want to show you something over in Red White's garage that his wife dragged home. You wouldn't believe some of the old junk she gets." Little did he suspect that the stove was his very own! A lot later, he admitted to liking it, and that same stove has a place of honor in our living room today. Some things one has to learn to love!

Loveta Wasson

November 15, 1985

Loveta Wasson, of Webster City, Iowa, is the mother of one of the teachers with whom I taught and socialized in La Porte City, Iowa, in 1939. The daughter, Mrs. Robert Moorman of Ames, and my sister Virginia are the only two (of six) bridesmaids at my wedding in 1941 who haven't died of cancer. Yes, we had twelve attendants at our church wedding and 350 persons at a sit-down dinner at long tables on our lawn at home.

My dad, being of simple Mennonite upbringing, thought perhaps we were going a little overboard, but Mom said, "You know Vera has always had loads of friends around, and we couldn't expect her to run off alone to be married."

Besides they were probably relieved, because I was such a late bloomer.

My nice brothers painted two signs on the honeymoon

car. One said, "We passed the test," and the other said, "Bride 24, Groom 21!"

Losing old friends

December 18, 1985

Usually I don't see old friends when we go to Denver, because we have so much family to see. This year I did see lots of my old friends because I was feeling maudlin about losing two of my best old friends last month—Billie Hines and Margaret Anderson, both sixty-one years old and both heavy smokers who died of lung cancer.

I'm feeling thankful now that I had a father who was an eye, ear, nose, and throat specialist and told me that smoking is bad for a person. I believed him to the extent that I never had one cigarette in my life. I wasn't even curious. I didn't care what they tasted like. Of course, my Dad also recommended being moderate in all things, including eating—which hasn't kept me from being obese.

Margaret Anderson, of La Jolla, California, twice invited all of the Colorado bridge retreat girls to be her guests at their oceanside condo, where she furnished all the food and took all twelve of us out to dinner every night we were there. She had attended the bridge retreat this past September at Estes Park, and she looked wonderful. In October she was hospitalized with pneumonia, and it was discovered that she had inoperable lung cancer. She died at home, and there was no funeral or memorial service. She was cremated and her ashes scattered over the Pacific Ocean.

That's the way I would prefer to depart, too. Undertakers claim that survivors need to have a funeral and to view the body to realize that their friends and loved ones are gone. Hogwash! If I didn't answer the phone, didn't show up at the post office to pick up my mail, and didn't attend any of my six fantastic bridge clubs, people could pretty well assume that I was dead!

Vera Smith on Vera Smith

On a stormy March night seventy-three years ago, I was born in the small Mennonite community of Kalona, Iowa, one of a family of four children. My father, Eli Stutsman, was a doctor who married my mother, Nina Shaver, the summer she graduated from high school. Theirs was a beautiful marriage that was to last fifty-three years. After graduating from the University of Northern Iowa, I taught at La Porte City, Iowa, for two years, where I met and married Courtney Kline. He was drafted into the military service in 1941, and I accompanied him around the United States as he served his country. We became the parents of two children and five grandchildren and lived in Denver, Colorado, for twenty-five years.

In 1967 we moved to a farm north of Glenwood, Iowa, where we discovered that my husband had terminal cancer. After his death, I taught at Lewis Central School in Council Bluffs, then married Rick Smith and moved to Malvern, Iowa, twenty years ago.

I started writing weekly columns entitled "Grannies Have More Fun" in 1976, when I became infuriated with all the put-downs and bad-mouthing to which we oldsters were being subjected daily. I've written over seven hundred two-page columns since then on the joys of being "middle-aged." My husband and I enjoy golf and enter husband/wife tournaments all over southwest Iowa. We love reading, hiking, gardening, antiquing, traveling, and playing bridge. With no parental interference and no live-in children for whom a good example must be set at all times, we feel that this is another carefree time of life— as good as the childhood years.